Commission
Checks

How to Close
More Real Estate Deals
and Deposit More Income

Tonja Demoff

KAPLAN) PUBLISHING

New York

This publication is designed to provide accurate and authoritative information in regard to the subject matter covered. It is sold with the understanding that the publisher is not engaged in rendering legal, accounting, or other professional service. If legal advice or other expert assistance is required, the services of a competent professional should be sought.

Vice President and Publisher: Maureen McMahon
Editorial Director: Jennifer Farthing
Acquisitions Editor: Michael Sprague
Production Editor: Karina Cueto
Cover Designer: Rod Hernandez
Typesetter: PBS & Associates

Published by Kaplan Publishing, a division of Kaplan, Inc.
1 Liberty Plaza, 24th Floor
New York, NY 10006

Printed in the United States of America

January 2008
10 9 8 7 6 5 4 3 2 1

ISBN-13: 978-1-4277-9591-5

Kaplan Publishing books are available at special quantity discounts to use for sales promotions, employee premiums, or educational purposes. Please email our Special Sales Department to order or for more information at kaplanpublishing@kaplan. com, or write to Kaplan Publishing, 1 Liberty Plaza, 24th Floor, New York, NY 10006.

To Carol and Barry: Thanks to your support, encouragement and genuine commitment to help your agents realize their dreams, I have discovered the most passionate side of my soul—all while accumulating a wealth of knowledge in the most nurturing environment imaginable.

To every real estate professional who desires to merge the creation of wealth with the intention to give back by selflessly serving the universe.

CONTENTS

Introduction

In *Commission Checks: How to Close More Real Estate Deals and Deposit More Income,* I hope to reach real estate agents who want to escalate their sales quotas in a fluctuating market. As a successful author, real estate broker and investor, business executive, and self-made multimillionaire, my approach is business-savvy, unique, and backed by my own accumulation of deposited commission checks! I hope you'll agree that I am in a position to educate other ambitious agents on how to reach a higher tax bracket.

Commission Checks teaches real estate agents how to increase their incomes and move away from their own shortcomings when putting together a deal. It outlines strategies for generating leads, setting the right intentions by identifying your goals and objectives by becoming more educated, and gaining the knowledge to explore more deal-closing options. In addition, this book emphasizes the importance of mastering the art of dealing with and working in sync with other real estate agents to sell their clients' points of view and put transactions together instead of pulling them apart.

To become successful agents with busy closing calendars, it is essential to learn how to control a deal without actually controlling it. Many times agents will forfeit a transaction because they are incapable of dealing with the listing or showing agent. Either they fail to communicate their client's position and requests effectively or they loose their composure, making them difficult to work with. A good closer does not allow personal feelings, attitudes, or opinions to get in the way. The transaction belongs to the client—not the agent.

Commission Checks stresses the importance of educating agents about how to avoid interfering in their own transactions so they can be open to effective communication. It explains how to design strategies that move forward towards a closing instead of in reverse.

Many agents believe that they know what they are doing when in reality they are totally clueless about the real estate process and their specific role as agents. They tend to speak from a position of unqualified authority when it would be wiser and more profitable to consult a professional, such as someone affiliated with the National Association of REALTORS® (NAR) who holds reputable credentials, or a real estate attorney.

An educated, well-informed agent inspires confidence and is more qualified to educate clients. A self-assured and knowledgeable agent puts together creative deals that are also beneficial to the seller. Moreover, those satisfied sellers and buyers are referral magnets—they will recommend a good professional to family and friends. It's a formula that works because the more knowledge you acquire, the more options you have, and the added options lead to increased earning.

Yet this book clears up the misconception many agents have regarding increased income. Earning more commission checks does not necessarily equate to closing more deals. *Commission Checks: How to Close More Real Estate Deals and Deposit More Income* addresses the fact that there are ways to earn more without having to conclude more transactions. It's not about working harder—it's about working smarter. It's about holding onto your commission as opposed to giving it up. Sometimes in a soft market, agents cut their own commissions, believing it is a sure way to get a listing. With this type of "negotiating," agents not only decrease their paychecks, but they also decrease their value as professionals. They work just as long and just as hard, but for a diminished compensation.

The pages to come answer the question on the tip of every agent's tongue: "How do I earn more substantial commissions, justify my value, and demonstrate to buyers and sellers that I am a qualified professional who warrants a six- or seven-percent commission agreement?"

When negotiating commissions, it is important not to steer the transaction downhill, even if you're not exactly working in a "bubble-proof" market. What is the point of getting an agent to list a property for a one- or two-percent commission, if it is going to sit on the market for a year or longer? This is certainly not profitable for the seller, who must continue to carry mortgage payments, insurance, property taxes, and homeowners' association fees. On the other hand, signing a listing agreement with an experienced, knowledgeable professional for a six-percent commission would guarantee a quicker sale.

I hope that the clear-cut presentation and theories outlined in *Commission Checks* opens the minds of agents to a whole new set of very different guidelines, encouraging them to ask the right questions before shooting down an offer without exploring all the facets of the transaction. My objective is for agents to have "no lives"—I want your calendars to be filled with closing appointments and trips to the bank—not endless showing dates and empty gas tanks.

This book addresses agents directly without frills or fancy rhetoric, asking the all-important question: "What is your real responsibility in selling property?" Many agents mistakenly undertake the role of decision maker for their clients. This misconception often leads to bad advice—this in turn trumps deals and commission checks.

Commission Checks is my "wake-up call" to agents. Yet I intend to do more than persuade agents to "wake up and smell the coffee"—they should "get up and sell the coffee shop!" This is accomplished through an informative, instructional, and easy-to-follow book—a book that focuses on reconfiguring mind-sets by disabling the virus-infested programming that crashes earning potential.

The challenge involves becoming properly educated. There is no company or organization that provides hands-on training for agents. Agents simply complete a course, take the test, and get their license, only to endure elongated listing periods, financial droughts, toxic stress, and bouts of frustration. The lucky ones may encounter a slow drizzle of commissions. Too many agents waste time learning through trial and error instead of collecting commission checks and building income assets.

Commission Checks creates savvy, successful agents. To me, it's more than a book—it is a real estate agent's bible—or at least the REALTORS®' *Gray's Anatomy*,—a multifaceted manual of instruction centered on offering agents an ivy-league-caliber education. Many may ask why I believe in well-educated agents. My answer is short and to the point; educated agents educate clients! It's all about the power of knowledge and its role in flipping leads into transaction agreeable clients. Simply put, it's about closing more deals and generating more income.

1

Depositing Commission Checks

Love What You Do—Defining the Agent's Role

*"It's tangible, it's solid, it's beautiful.
It's artistic, from my standpoint,
and I just love real estate."*

—Donald Trump

Motivation and inspiration set the stage for building profit-centered strategies that transform a mediocre real estate agent into an exceptional, high-powered "closing" phenomenon. The key to achieving this goal is adapting a winning mind-set and knowing from the start that the way to be phenomenal is to focus on being of service to your client. In other words, it's your client's deal—not yours!

It is however, your responsibility as an agent to represent your clients. Be sensitive to their needs and always request and work accordingly in their best interests. Representation is synonymous with communication. Talk to them, ask questions, and learn who they are and what they want. Let them tell you what they are looking for. Don't nominate yourself to be their spokesperson. Instead be an investigator —get to know their mind-set and what it is they expect from you as their representative in the home-buying process. Then learn to define and evaluate your part in the equation.

Ask yourself if you want to become a top-notch agent. Before putting together a transaction, it is important to have a clear definition of your role. In determining this factor, be certain not to cross over the boundary between realtor® and client. Understanding your position and focusing your mind-set on serving your clients solidifies your objectivity and prevents you from operating in a subjective style.

Many agents never rise from the ranks of mediocrity because they are "right-brain" thinkers who base their assessments and judgments on intuition. These emotion-driven agents usually dive into the big picture while overlooking the small but important details. Consequently they make personal, emotional decisions that are not necessarily in the best interest of their clients.

Over and over throughout my two-decade career in real estate, I've listened to the verbiage of agents who use a philosophy similar to: "Well, I don't want to get my client into that type of deal because if he agrees, then it won't be in his best interest." My response is immediate: "How do you know it is not in the client's best interest?"

What's happening here is that the agent is removing the decision-making ability from the client and putting it where it doesn't belong— in the hands of the agent. This is a mind-set based on personal perspective and opinion. If, as an agent, you feel a transaction may not be in your best interest, then you will automatically transfer that method of reasoning to your client. Therefore you will treat the transaction as a less than good prospect when in reality it could be a profitable deal. In the end everyone loses—no sale for the client and no commission check for you.

REI—Real Estate Investigator

You need to be an investigator and take the time to interview your client. Open a discussion by saying, "Let's talk about what you're looking for." Then ask:

- Are you a loft or condo person?
- Are you looking for proximity to top-tier educational facilities?
- Do you want a child-friendly neighborhood?
- How can I best serve you and your needs?
- Would you like me to help you find your ideal house?
- What do you think about this property?
- How will these terms and/or conditions work for you?

Your client's answers will provide what you need to get a winning transaction and, at the same time, the client will feel in control of the situation.

Client-Agent Communication

Keep the pipeline clear. Often when agents fail to communicate with clients, they end up with buyers who may be conditioned by what they consider a "professional opinion." The agents feel trapped, believing if they contradict the "expert's" point of view, they could offend the client or embarrass themselves. Many times I've heard, "Well he is the Realtor," or "the broker said this condo acquisition transaction would not be financially profitable for me and she's been in the business a long time. Anyway I need the money right now for my daughter's surgery."

Consequently, without even exploring other financial avenues, the client walks away from a deal that may have been not only a successful transaction, but also a great investment. The seller remains without an offer and the REALTOR® loses a sale due to negligence in not taking the time to listen to the client. Consequently there is no commission check to deposit and no potential for building a satisfied client referral database.

The bottom line is nobody wins. More importantly this counter-productive behavior pattern creates the limiting bottlenecks that breed "milk and water agents," trapping them in mediocrity—if not buried in failure. Why be chattel when you can be real property?

Breaking the No-Win Cycle

The first step to breaking this no-win cycle is to prioritize—the client takes precedence over everything else. Once this part of the equation is unraveled, it is vital to understand every facet of the volatile real estate market, not just the ritual of passing back and forth the paper pyramid of listing agreements, sales contracts, deeds, disclosure forms, mortgage agreements, real estate installment agreements, and affidavits.

Accumulating an abundance of commission checks and leveraging efficiency as an agent is dependent on being real estate savvy. That means knowing more than bureaucratic procedure and the less-than-phenomenal marketing tips and techniques shared in the REALTOR® guidelines. Educated agents move beyond business strategies that involve contacting expired listings and for-sale-by-owner properties. Informed agents go directly to the hub of the business. They get to the core, gather facts and figures, and familiarize themselves with every aspect of the buying and selling procedure, earning credibility while differentiating their credentials from those of mediocre agents.

How to Win at the REALTOR® Game

In my opinion a winning agent has mastered the escrow process and is familiar with the different types of title:

- Chain of title—trace ownership
- Clear title—free from lien
- Clouded title—an unreleased lien or impediment that could hinder a title to a property

I believe in self-education. I am convinced it is the combination that opens the vault of success. An agent who is continually evolving, learning, growing, and researching how to do it better is the agent striving to be number one—the winner in his or her profession. The only way real estate agents and all independent contractors can increase their financial universe is to broaden and gain control of their knowledge.

Enhancing real estate education requires:

- Researching, interviewing, and pulling together a top-notch team of experts
- Listening to the professionals
- Moving beyond the world of podcasts, flippant bloggers dispensing amateur "how-to" tips in the global blogsphere, and inadequate brochures powered by insignificant bullet tips
- Specializing and fine tuning your knowledge
- Asking questions; picking the brains of CPAs, tax attorneys, title reps, 1031 tax specialists, and property and termite companies
- Being thorough in your pursuit of information

In addition to assembling a team of experts, it is also important to become fully acquainted with homeowners' associations (HOA) and club equity requirements if the property in a transaction is part of a subdivision or development. Many clients—especially those downsizing from single-family dwellings—may be confused or unfamiliar with the HOA process. If a client asks a question, you should be able to respond clearly and knowledgeably in order to build confidence and quash any doubt or reservation that could spring from lack of information and prevent the deal from closing.

Success Empowerment

Once you have clearly delineated your boundaries, educated yourself, and nurtured your mind-set to enhance and empower your journey to success, you must have faith in your ability to perform. You will not achieve if you do not believe in yourself, just as you will never realize an objective if you don't first visualize it. The key words are:

- Believe—Achieve
- Visualize—Realize

It's a good mantra to repeat daily in order to keep you oriented toward success.

Start by setting a goal. Ask yourself:

- How do I want to be of service?
- How can I be on top of the competition by going one step beyond?
- How can I make a difference in my business?

Before you can respond to your own interrogations, you must design a business model, create strategies, and devise a method to put it all into action. For instance, if you hold a California license, don't limit your business exclusively to a 60-mile radius in Orange County. Branch out—get knowledgeable about market value, investment opportunities, and listed properties in San Francisco or San Diego. Think big—browse the MLS, broaden the panorama, step into the big picture, and earn more commission checks without leaving Orange County through the building of a substantial referral base.

Major League Agents Versus Little League Agents

For some agents, playing in the major leagues for sizeable commission checks may be too intimidating. They just can't get their arms around this big-picture strategy. It's too overwhelming. However, many "little league" agents are good farmers who specialize in a limited area. They focus on farming 200 homes and become experts in that region. The secret is to find a business model that fits your own intentions and objectives. If your feet are small, don't try to walk in size 12 shoes. You will just trip over your feet and end up with your nose in the mud! Knowing your own boundaries will keep you grounded.

Defining the terms and scope of your business model allows you to concentrate and specialize either in specific neighborhoods or broad-scale multi-cities. This is an individual preference with which each agent must come to terms. Personally, I am the kind of professional who would be bored farming a restricted area. Instead I have a macro perspective on life—I prefer to play in the major league and chart, strategize, and execute my business model accordingly.

I can now hang on my wall real estate licenses from 10 different states—for me, this is exciting, challenging, and empowering. Selling in multiple states gets me jetting around the country. My travel expenses are filtered through tax deductions—and all while I enjoy myself, visit new cities and towns, and make money. I bring my profit-centered self to life and get paid for what I love to do. This in turn gives me a green light to continue doing what I love. It's a win-win situation!

Broadening Professional Horizons

It doesn't end with the licenses currently hanging on my wall. While some agents have told me they were only willing to walk five blocks to deliver their services, I'm always open to broadening my professional horizons. The reason other agents tread along the narrow path is that they know the community and feel at an advantage in familiar territory. Although limited-boundary agents can be successful, this is not the philosophy of an exceptional agent. To gain phenomenal status and have a remarkable profit center you must:

- Do what you love to do in a way that is not overwhelming.
- Feel in control of your business.
- Be able to manage every aspect of it.

When people become snowed-under their diminished profitability quotient leads to stagnation. With too many responsibilities, they freeze and become immobile. That's bad for business.

Balancing the Success Equation

An important element needed to balance the success equation is the ability to find ways to incorporate what you love to do into the real estate business. For example, as a frequent traveler and a "people person," I am a great resource for referrals. I have created and continue to expand a vast network of agents in diverse cities and states. I could be in Nevada or California and send a client to Florida or even the Virgin Islands, where I have a reputable agent qualified to help them acquire the property they desire.

The key is to find opportunities to do what you love.

- Don't dwell on one aspect of the business.
- Broaden your focus.
- Be open to finding other avenues to explore. A single-stream income should not be the end result.
- Create multiple revenue streams.
- Ask yourself, "How can I create profit centers within my company?"

Income Revenue

There are various sources of income revenue in the real estate business:

- Commission checks
- Referral income
- Lease options—Many agents snub lease options because if they sell a property today, then they may not get paid until the option is exercised. Although this may occur a year down the line, it is earning potential. Immediate gratification is not always the only road to the bank.
- Loan process—Some companies are equipped to generate revenue by receiving compensation from the broker or agent. Being able to visualize, create, and manage various opportunities is a lucrative income-growing strategy. If you get a commission check and compensation for a loan process, one transaction has netted you two paychecks.

One of the keys to multi-income resources is communication. It is often given little credence as a way to generate more income yet it cannot be stressed enough. Communication puts a higher premium on listening rather than speaking. Most agents want to tell the listing agent what their client is willing to do or not do in order to complete the transaction. Yet, if they listened more and asked the other agent pertinent questions, they could find the opportunity to put the deal together instead of pulling it apart.

Ask and Listen Strategy

Whether you are the listing broker or showing agent, the objective is not only to ask more questions but also, above all, to *listen* to the answers. Listening is an income enhancer. In so doing, you acquire more knowledge about the buyer and seller and learn what it takes to make or break a deal. Once you fully understand the needs and requirements of a buyer and seller, you can devise a more powerful and profitable negotiating strategy.

Many agents unconsciously "tip their cards" during negotiations. Often an agent will emphatically tell me his clients are absolutely not going to agree to hold the property because they were just relocated out of state and cannot afford not to sell their house, nor will they adjust their price. Well, that's just nuts! The agent's clients are surely willing to drop the price because of the two reasons the agent revealed: It's an out-of-state relocation and the clients are not in a financial position to hang on to the property. If the agent had listened more closely to his clients, then he would have had a closing instead of an unsigned purchase agreement.

Outline and Communicate Technique

My technique when dealing with other agents is to communicate in more than just a verbal format. For instance, to be certain I have clarified every point initially discussed I document every agreement finalized over the phone in a "based on our phone conversation it is my understanding…" email. Putting the terms of the agreement in writing avoids the risk of error and misunderstanding between agents.

When communicating with another agent about an impending transaction, it is important to keep in mind who you represent. Often the only issue on the agents' minds is the commission check. The needs and requests of the client are shifted into second place. The agents parley between each other with tactics to benefit themselves. They ask, "How do you think we can get this deal done? Is your client willing to come up because if your client will, then maybe I can also get mine to come down." They throw out numbers regarding what they think their clients will sign a purchase agreement for. This is clearly not client representation.

In almost two decades of asking agents what they think the seller will take in order to close the deal, I have received almost exclusively "right-brain" responses. One agent told me off the top of his head that it would take $375,000 to get a closing date. If the agent would have at least quoted full price he would have demonstrated some concern for his client. Instead he negotiated his own price, totally discounting the wishes and intentions of the seller.

REALTOR® Ethics

Buyers and sellers must feel comfortable working with you. They want and deserve a knowledgeable professional who exercises her profession with integrity and focuses her objectives exclusively on the interest of the client. Buyers and sellers must hold you in high esteem for your professionalism and principled work ethic. In essence, as an agent you are simply the person who is transferring information and guiding clients, as well as assisting a buyer or seller in making the decision that will lead them to a successful outcome—a deal closing.

When REALTORS® take on the role of decision maker they loose a lot of deals—and a lot of money! Our profession is about respect— it's about allowing the client to be in command of his financial and personal choices. During negotiations, if an agent says, "I don't think this would work for you," then she is making an unsolicited judgment call. This unprofessional behavior diminishes the client's role as primary decision maker in the selling or acquisition of personal property.

Often clients do not list their properties with the agents who sold it to them. Curious, isn't it? When asked why, they often respond that they really didn't like their previous agent. When pressed further, often the clients were dissatisfied with the agent because they didn't think he was professional. The agent was much too opinionated—it was all about him.

It's Not About You—It's About the Client

On a recent trip to Aspen, Colorado, I contacted a local agent and created a referral agreement with him for a fifty-fifty commission split. Then I flew out to buy 18 properties that I had researched and found prior to my arrival. He spent about five hours driving around, showing me the properties, which ranged in price from an $800,000 condo to an $8 million house. I brought 18 buyers to the table.

The agent accompanied me to preview the properties. He had something to say about each one. When he turned the key and opened the door to the first condo we visited, he said, "This one is great—it's my favorite. It has an awesome mountain view! It is my absolute favorite —that's why I picked it!"

En route to the next property, he wrinkled his nose and told me that he really didn't like the place, emphasizing that it was his least favorite, and he really didn't see any value in it. Consequently, immediately, even before previewing the property, I had lost interest because, willingly or otherwise, he had conditioned me to dislike it. Thankfully I persisted and when we stepped inside, I realized it was a fabulous property.

When I asked the agent why he didn't like the property, his response was filled with personal comments such as, "I like a bit more light here and I want it darker there." The answer was a list of his personal house-buying criteria.

This right-brained agent expressed an opinion about each of the 18 properties before he actually turned the key. It was more than apparent to me that he knew nothing about client representation. It was all about his likes and dislikes—but he wasn't the buyer!

Instead of taking the subjective approach, he should have kept his opinions to himself and listened to the needs and wants of his client. Once he had a good picture concerning what to look for to best satisfy his client's wants, he would have been in a better position to advise and decide what properties would have qualified for selling potential. There is a difference between advising, deciding, and conditioning; just as there is a difference between a signed purchase agreement and an unsigned or revoked one.

The whole experience was quite hilarious to me. I was certain this man was not and would not be "agent of the year" in his company unless he changed his method of doing business.

I had a similar experience while previewing properties in Ohio. In each house, the agent opened the door and began to direct me around room by room, explaining where the kitchen, bathroom, and family room were situated. Then after the "tour," she turned on her heel, changed direction, pointed her finger, and informed me that the master suite and backyard were at the opposite end.

As I neared the bathroom, she proceeded to tell me that I was nearing the bathroom and that a walk-in closet was nearby. The only thing she accomplished was getting a chuckle out of me for the thought that perhaps in her mind, I was incapable of distinguishing between a kitchen and a master suite, or that I might confuse a bathroom with the backyard!

Northstrom Approach

Even an amateur agent should realize this is not a winning approach. Instead of cataloging each room, she would have been better off following the Northstrom approach and telling her clients:

- Go ahead and feel free to look around the property.
- If you have any questions, please don't hesitate to ask.
- I'm just going to walk around and open all the windows so you can see how light and bright it can be.

Use Your Imagination

Invite the clients to enjoy their stroll around the property. Give them space to envision themselves there. Stop chattering (it is difficult to think in a chaotic environment), and enable them to set their imaginations in motion.

- Adjust your style to the circumstances.
- Be inviting, but keep quiet.

- Let the clients roam around and familiarize themselves with the surroundings.

If people are unable to visualize living in a home or condo, then they are unlikely to buy it. Once again, no sale—and no commission check to deposit.

My style sometimes involves asking the agent if they would mind not talking while I'm previewing. I like to go to the property and just look and walk around. I need to take it in because I buy properties intuitively and based upon my gut feeling. I don't want to know the statistics, the comps, or the data, until I get a feel for it. When the vibe I'm looking for happens, I move to the next step. I do a head check to determine if my intellect is in sync with my intuition. If I get a green light on both sides, then I move forward.

Structure a Business Plan

Once again, the way to become a phenomenal agent is to be attuned not with yourself but with your client. It is also important to structure a business plan. Not all clients are created equally. We live in a world of difference and diversity. Study individual expectations and needs. Some clients fare better with daily contact regarding available property, whereas others welcome neither phone calls nor emails until you have found exactly what they are looking for.

When meeting new clients, run through a checklist of questions to determine what type of property would satisfy their needs and requirements. At the end of the questioning, ask them how you could best serve them and how they wish to proceed with the house-buying process. Listen to their responses and design your strategy accordingly.

Recently I was in a situation outside of real estate that echoed this process. I had decided to hire a personal trainer. In order to finalize my decision, I phoned him to see if he would be the right man for the job. During the initial moments of our conversation, he was straightforward and told me he would only assume me as a client if I agreed to work his way. I asked him to define "his way" and he told me that if I was willing to commit to working out with him, I had to keep my appointments. If for any reason I would be unable to and failed to give him a 24-hour cancellation notice, I would be charged for the forfeited session. Furthermore, if I missed more than five sessions in a six-month period, then he would drop me as a client.

Immediately I knew he was the trainer for me. In my opinion, he's a professional who knows exactly how he wants to do business. His business strategy is clearly defined and his determination to uphold his method is commendable. I realized that working with this trainer would leave me without flexibility. In this specific type of "transaction," it is a positive because his service involves something (exercise and fitness training) that the client cannot do without. The discipline he proposes is a key factor to success.

When selling a home or investment property, a rigid disciplinarian strategy would result in a no-show. My trainer is so steadfast and inflexible in his approach that he forfeits half his clients every year, but because he has decided that he only wants to focus his efforts on people who are serious and keep their appointments, he is not concerned about the clients he loses. His priorities include beneficial utilization of his time, in lieu of squandering it on motivationally dysfunctional people.

In real estate, agents have to understand that if they are going to make a decision to be a *bona fide* hardnose and dictate how clients are going to conduct business, then they have to be prepared to have less clients—and that is not always a negative. However, to be successful with less, the clients must be multitransactional. In other words, they must have more buying and selling power.

My clients do multiple transactions because my approach to business dips more toward inflexible than flexible, although I am very service-oriented. I have a business model that does not favor starter-home buyers. Instead of turning them away, I refer them to other agents in my network who are equipped to suit their needs.

Consistency is a vital factor when devising a business model. Define your style and approach and stick to it. I know I work well with investors and absolutely cannot work with first-time home-buyers. Sometimes clients who I refer to other agents phone me and say that they prefer to work with me. My response is honest and up front.

"No you really don't," I say, "and let me tell you why. I don't have any patience. I'm not a first-time homebuyer and if you walked into a house I knew had $50,000 worth of profit and you absolutely hated it because the carpet was red, I would flip. My reaction would be to tell you to buy the house and get a new carpet!"

I am not an agent who would tell you that if this house does not meet your emotional needs, then we'll look for 40 more properties. Instead, I am the type of broker who gets on the MLS, prints every available property in a client's price range, hands the client the sheets, and tells her to drive to all of them. When the client finds five that excite her, then we'll look at them so the choices can be narrowed down. We'll pick one and we can close.

Usually, my referrals will laugh and roll their eyes at me, but my message is serious: I don't want to deprive them of the opportunity to buy the home they desire, especially their first one.

Property Acquisition Process

House-buying can be a very emotional process because:
- It's built on private ownership.
- It's motivated by personal opinions and feelings.
- The decision is not typically based on an investment strategy.

Some people, whether they are first-time or one-time buyers or sellers or seasoned investors, will be willing to look at it from my perspective and agree to try it my way. Before we do business, I outline my strategy:
- I show only five properties.
- The client will have to get another agent if none of the five is suitable.
- I'll provide all of the necessary information to find and tour the properties.
- Clients are free to attend any open house.
- Clients are free to call any listing agent, however the buyer's agreement remains.
- Clients can find their own properties.
- I will help with the negotiations.

My business model may be somewhat rigid, but I have never lost a client to another agent. In fact, sometimes my clients phone and inform me they found a FSBO and ask is there something I can do to get my commission! Instinctively I tell them, "You bet I can!" If I can't negotiate a commission, I'll still get them the property—but it's my fault if I'm not knowledgeable enough to close the deal thus forfeiting the commission.

Establishing set guidelines for your business model will contribute to your success. Knowing how you plan to do business and with what type of client you work best are essential factors. Many agents fail in the earning department because they grab any deal that comes along and try to figure it out. For instance, if an investor calls with the intent to purchase a $10 million piece of commercial property and the agent has never done anything except residential transactions, then most likely the end result will be no closing, no commission check, and a lot of wasted time and energy.

The smart agent will decide not to work with properties outside of his knowledge or experience. Instead, the agent will utilize his time and energy to create a referral network with professionals who handle commercial properties.

A winning strategy involves being open to opportunities, but not so open that greed entices you to work alone and fail at what you are attempting to accomplish. Always remember to:

- Know your strengths and weaknesses.
- Work with your talents.
- Do what you are good at.
- Evolve—change from a middle-of-the-road agent into a high-powered profit center in command of your financial universe.

It's about flipping your time and energy into substantial commission checks and depositing more income.

2

Don't Trip over Your Feet

"The ego is not master in its own house."

—Sigmund Freud

People who allow their egos to dominate their lives and control their decisions are motivated by fear. In real estate, being fearful translates to poverty. The ego is our nemesis—it fights with other agents and prohibits buyers and sellers from making their own decisions. If an agent has to be the source of authority in a transaction and is more concerned with being perceived in a certain way, then the deal will be thwarted by that mind-set.

On the other hand, if agents take on the willingness to be helpful and move toward a closing, they will proceed forward to a positive end result instead of stopping the deal before it starts. In every transaction I have been involved in, if the deal fails to close on the scheduled day

I get a phone call from the listing agent asking me why the deal didn't close as scheduled. In rebuttal, I ask if all of that agent's deals close on time. Most agents will respond in the affirmative, claiming they have a pretty good success rate. When asked to define pretty good, however, they look into the air and mutter a percentage figure that comes off the top of their heads and has no relevance in truth.

Deal-Closing Flexibility

During my almost two decades of experience in the real estate business, I have found that most deals do not close on time. Therefore, when a postponement occurs, I do not freak out and phone the other agent with threats and complaints (though many agents aren't above that kind of intimidation tactic). Many agents use a negative ego force based on fear—they are afraid if they don't proceed aggressively that they will be deprived of their commission. Their follow-up involves harassing the lender with daily phone calls and emails. Taking it a step further, they then bombard me with calls. When this happens the only word I have for them is *desperate*.

I think to myself that agents who resort to these tactics must be broke because they seem to have such a surplus of time and attention to dedicate to one transaction in such an annoying and unproductive way. This behavior tells me they will not get the commission simply because the very thing they fear will happen will because they were too afraid to let go of their ego.

Fear—The Deal Breaker

More deals fall apart when agents become so riddled in fear that they use a manipulative strategy they learned as children—the fight or flight response. This is a mechanism activated by the overwhelming stress resulting from a perception of threatened survival. In real estate, this occurs when:

1. An agent sees a deal going down the drain.
2. Fright moves in, and she rolls up the sales agreement.
3. The agent tucks it under her arm.
4. She nullifies it.
5. Flight takes over and the agent walks away from the table.

The agent's reaction emulates the behavior of children in a disagreement with playmates. At the first sign of conflict, these agents gather up their marbles and flee. Often the same faulty thinking allows agents to believe that such childish conduct will get them what they want. This could not be further from the truth—deals are not closed as a result of "agent tantrums."

The second option to the fight or flight response is the confrontational approach. When a deal seems headed in a wrong direction, agents become combative, arguing with the listing agents to compensate for the threat of a lost commission check. Bickering has never generated a sale. Therefore, either response—fight or flight—is counterproductive and triggered exclusively by a negatively focused ego.

Agent Objectivity

Successful agents are willing and able to shift this unconstructive belief and position their ego in the direction of a positive outcome. Emotional decisions and judgments are the exclusive "property" of the buyers and sellers. Agents have a responsibility to relay information to their clients in an objective and professional way that does not fuel excessive emotions by repeating what other agents and the buyers and sellers said about a given property or deal.

Buyers and sellers should not even be aware of the issues agents discuss among themselves. This type of feedback serves only to empower a transaction with a stream of negative energy while conditioning the major players.

When an unnecessary discussion ensues between the involved parties, it's best to walk away. The information "ping-pong" is a drawback to the outcome of the deal. Once a "leaky faucet" has dripped water, the transaction is damaged.

As an agent, my role in the transaction is either advocate or pen-pushing bureaucrat—a nonaligned participant who passes information from one side to another in the most professional manner possible, being attentive to keep the door closed to my personal opinions. What I think and how I feel about a property are irrelevant. Remember:

- It's all about the buyer and the seller.
- It's about what *they* think and how *they* feel.

Setting Productive Intentions

Instead of nurturing your ego set your intentions on moving toward your client's purpose. If they want to close on a property, your objective is to work toward bringing the transaction to a positive outcome. If they are intent on walking away from a deal, then your goal is to move toward a cancellation. In other words, the client guides your strategy.

This same mind-set can be applied to structuring a commission. An agent's attitude translates to either a substantial or insignificant check. Experience has taught me that agents who are overly aggressive and combative are prone to negotiating price-reduction commissions because they are motivated by fears such as:

- They are afraid of not getting listings.
- They fear a depleted earning.
- They are scared other agents will be open to dropping their commission a percent point or more in order to snatch listing agreements.

This leads to commission competition without any regard for professional value.

Professional Value and Commission Percentage

An agent's professional value is calculated by the quality of service provided to a client. When agents ask me how they can put a number on their professional worth, I tell them that the best way to estimate their value is by assessing their bank accounts.

Some of my clients are willing to pay me as much as 15 or 20 percent on a real estate transaction without blinking twice. They'll pay it because they know the quality of service I'm willing to offer. I don't just grab the listing, put it on the MLS, and then sit at Starbucks attached to my Bluetooth earpiece and wireless notebook, sipping a latte while other agents show and "push" my listings.

My quality of service involves structuring a package deal that upon request will put my clients in contact with a tax attorney, a CPA, and a 1031 specialist. In synthesis I am their information resource, and sufficiently educated to be able to assist them both with their financial plan, and the actual transition to a new property.

I accomplish this goal because my business model involves demonstrating to clients how they can pay me the commission I deserve, save taxes, and obtain the finances they need to close the deal. When clients understand an agent is committed to working on their behalf and has priceless resources to share, then they know they have an agent who brings enormous value to the table. They also realize that such a powerhouse professional is worth the commission negotiated and they are more than willing to pay it without any doubts or reservations. However, they are livid—as they should be—if they have to shell out even a one-percent commission to an agent who is lax, indifferent, or uninvolved, demonstrates little professionalism, and possesses no interpersonal skills.

My clients know that my minimum commission is a nonnegotiable 10 percent because whenever I'm asked to reduce a commission, my answer is simple and direct: "I'm very good at what I do; therefore I pay myself very well." In essence what they are paying for is the expertise I bring to the process, and the top of the line service I'm committed to offering. If they inform me they are unwilling to meet my financial requirements, I simply say: "I understand and appreciate your position. Personally I am not willing to negotiate my commission, but I would be more than happy to refer you to an agent who is more flexible."

Usually I find they are agreeable to working with someone else because the financial aspect of the transaction is an uncompromising priority for them. On my part, by referring the deal to another agent, I create a stream of revenue for myself even without handling the deal. The client is satisfied and I come out ahead of the game.

Agent Savvy

Put your ego away! I practice what I preach and always put my clients' needs first. If they tell me it's totally about the money and they have to get as much out of this transaction as they can, then I reassure them that it's my objective to meet all their conditions. My next move is to recommend a for-sale-by-owner (FSBO) option. If a client expresses that they want as much as possible financially then why even suggest an agent? Statistically speaking, the for-sale-by-owner approach nets less than an ideal outcome for the REALTOR®, and without a seller-agent monetary agreement, there is a good possibility that no agent will drive a client to the front door of an unlisted property. Regardless of how ethically driven a professional may be, without a financial compensation, the property becomes "off limits." In addition, most agents are familiar only with homes on the MLS, listed in the classifieds, posted on craigslist, or "advertised" on lawn signs stuck in the grass along the roads they travel to and from work and/or social activities. In others words, they don't go out of their way.

Agents have to stand on solid ground and know the value they bring to a transaction. When attending a listing presentation, it is important to walk in feeling confident and fully prepared. Fully prepared doesn't mean being able to rattle off the comps, discuss market value, and give a verbal tour of the neighborhood's assets. It means being able to handle the unspoken questions. The inquiries that often spring forth may be many and various, such as:

- How many properties have you sold?
- How long have you been in the business?
- What sets you apart from others?
- Why will you be able to sell my property faster than another agent will?

A client's mind is always seeking an answer to the money questions such as:

- What real estate company can get me top dollar for my house?
- Which agent will find what I want quickly and on my terms?

Get informed and be ready to use your knowledge to get the listing.

- Learn why you are the person for the job.
- Discover why you excel in your profession—pinpoint your strengths.
- Learn how to communicate your professional ability to clients in a credible manner.
- Have documented facts to back up your agent savvy status.

Reaching for the Listings— Determining Market Value

Some clients will list with the agent who puts their property in the highest price range. Many times I have heard sellers say, "I'm listing my house with Century 21 because they valued it at six million dollars—that's 15 percent higher than the last property that sold on my street."

Refuse this type of strategizing; if that seller tells me he spoke with another agent from a different company who came back with an elevated appraisal figure, and the seller wants to set this figure as his asking price, I tell the seller that *there is a possibility* that he can get $6 million—in fact maybe even $8 million! I certainly don't have a crystal ball—and no one knows for sure how much the property will go for.

Market value is established in accordance with certain factors:

- The desire of the buyer
- What she is willing to pay for a property
- The market comps categorizing the last property sold in the same neighborhood

Although I may think a client's property is worth only $5,150,000, I would be willing to list it for whatever amount the client wishes if he agrees to my demands. The conditions would include his signature on an agreement stipulating that if there is no activity on the home and if we get no offers within a reasonable period of time that we define, then we will automatically and simultaneously do a price reduction and an extension of the listing agreement.

The end result is the appropriate amount of time within which to have the opportunity to sell the house for the appropriate market value, without any flack from the client because I hold a long-term nonactive listing.

Believe It—Achieve It

As I said earlier, no one has a crystal ball so no one can accurately predict how a property will sell. Price and time frame are all unknowns, just numbers on a spinning roulette wheel.

Not long ago I listed one of my properties for $1 million over the market value. Every agent in Corona Del Mar, where the property was located, contacted me personally to inform me my asking price was bordering on ridiculous. I am not exaggerating when I say that about 30 agents bombarded me with phone calls. The calls were all the same: they shouted that the price was absolutely outrageous and that the last comp in that area was $1 million lower.

To each and every "concerned" caller I said that I was sorry he or she felt that way, nonetheless I was convinced my property had an additional $1 million worth of value. I said that simply because there was no comparable due to a minus sales record in the development didn't mean it had no market value. It just meant I didn't have a comp to base my listed value on because there were no sales during the past year in that development. I explained that 18 months ago I purchased the property for $1 million less.

In this situation, I'm going to establish the market value. If there is a buyer willing to pay $1 million more, then the new figure becomes a comp. That being the case, certainly everyone in the development would be ecstatic—as their properties just appreciated *en masse.*

Most of the agents listened and hung up, still believing I was nuts, but I held firm. Soon after, I received four offers on the property—all were about $800,000 or so below my asking price—and all were rejected. Then I received a full-price, all-cash offer with a 30-day closing date. I knew I was in business—an all-cash transaction, one month until closing, and for $1 million more than I paid.

When the agents saw the sale in the MLS my phone rang off the hook again. This time they shouted, "We never would have believed it!"

Those words confirmed my theory that they could never have sold the property because in order to have closed the deal, an agent would have had to believe it was possible to get the asking price despite it all.

Hold firm to your conviction: If you want to achieve, you must believe.

Doing Business Your Way

When a client tells you she thinks her property is worth $2 million, tell her that it's okay if that's her gut feeling, but you should protect yourselves. If you're going to invest time and energy into listing and marketing her house, then you need some reassurance that she won't hold it against you if her gut feeling is wrong and she thinks she can turn a $750,000 home into a $2 million property.

You don't want her to be furious when four months down the line the property remains on the market—without even a pending status. If it sells, wonderful—and you should do everything in your power to get her asking price, but based on a statistical time line reporting how long it takes to sell a property, and how long sellers have to wait, she and you need to be realistic if these conditions are not reasonable. Therefore you need to enter into an agreement.

A suitable time line for a listing depends on:

- The results of a market analysis that determines how long other area properties in a similar price range sit uncontracted
- The seller's exigencies if there are no comps and the agent is trying to establish a market value
- When the client needs to sell
- When the client chooses to sell
- How long the client is willing to hold off until getting her price
- Whether or not the client is willing to wait for a listed price contract (If the client is willing to wait and the agent demands the client's asking price, then both agent and seller should be willing to wait it out. My mantra is list it high and list it long!)

Commission Negotiating

In the previously mentioned situation, you are taking a $2 million listing for a property that you believe to be valued at $750,000. Personally I would take at minimum a one-year listing and preferably a two-year. Rushing the process often results in tripping over your feet, as does negotiating a commission to a below-par one percent and working for petty cash.

If an agent has a listing for a one-percent commission, he must be aware that in most states the REALTOR® has the right to negotiate the percentage. In other words, just because the agreement stipulates one percent doesn't mean it's an immoveable locked-in rate.

I have real estate companies in several Florida cities and find it rather interesting working in the Southeast. When I began working in that region there seemed to be a double standard. The properties were listed with a one-percent commission but at the closing table I discovered it was actually six percent. However, the listing agent was only giving out one percent and keeping the other five percent—a kind of one-sided business arrangement favoring one agent in the transaction. Strange as it may seem, this commission strategy was widespread in Florida. Once I understood the *modus operandi,* I began to negotiate my commissions up to three and four percent.

The Florida agents told me I could not negotiate because it's already predetermined. This response did not sit well with me—nor should it with you!

I said that I would not accept their way of doing business and asked them to show me where it specifies that negotiating a commission is prohibited. In my opinion, a nonnegotiable transaction would be price-fixing. As a matter of fact, in California there is a commission negotiation form to make certain the agreement exists between the listing and showing agents and not the buyers and sellers. It is a separate document, which is not part of the sales contract.

Negotiating commissions gives successful professionals who have neither disciplinary actions against them nor lengthy inactive sales periods the edge over mediocre agents. They can command a higher rate based on a phenomenal performance record in a short period of time.

Still, it is important to understand the methods of effective negotiating. If agents are previewing properties and automatically rejecting deals with one- or two-percent commissions, then they are in reality limiting their business potential—especially in a buyer's market. Too many agents use a commission-reduction tactic believing it is synonymous with more deals and additional commission checks, but this is just another form of limiting your income. The name of the game is "commission negotiating."

If a listing agent is able to gain the confidence of a seller, the commission negotiation process stands on firmer ground. After all, the success of a transaction is based on finding a buyer—this is the most difficult part of the deal, and the part that belongs to the listing agent. Therefore the listing agent comes to the table with an ace in hand: "Give me a four- to five-percent commission, and I'll bring the buyer to the door."

Effective negotiating can also be based on the sales strategy. If an agent has a serious buyer and can close without the involvement of another agent, he can negotiate a better commission deal because there are no splits and the listing broker can reasonably claim a higher percentage.

Tripping over Your Own Feet

Other impediments to depositing commission checks are the deal-breaking verbal slipups to which some agents are prone. They may be innocent *faux pas* but they often result in devastating consequences. An example of a deal-breaking blunder would be an agent tipping his cards by telling another broker or the seller how far his client is willing to negotiate. An agent gives away too much by offering common phrases like, "My client is very motivated." So many agents have tripped over their own feet by putting their foot in their mouths.

To keep from tripping, agents must learn the value of keeping their personal opinions under lock and key. As egoistical, knowledgeable,

and self-assured agents can be, the truth is that their views and consid-
erations are dually insignificant and irrelevant in the buying and selling
of property.

Often an agent will walk into a house and recite a theatrical litany
of praise: "Oh, just look how wonderful this place is! What a fabulous
layout it has! Look at the spacious family room. What a fantastic view!
And what a lively neighborhood—so close to the best high school in
the city!"

In the meantime, the clients find the same house less-than-
wonderful. They feel the layout is unaccommodating to their lifestyle,
they don't find the mountain view relaxing, and they fear that living in
proximity to a school would be less than tranquil as a result of traffic
jams and pollution from school buses riding up and down the street
several times a day. After the agent's burst of enthusiasm, they see the
emotional display to be Act 1 of a less-than-convincing sales pitch by
an agent with poor taste. As a result, the potential buyers are turned off
to the property—and more importantly, to the agent.

Perhaps a client asks if the house is near a hospital, and because the
agent has a diabetic partner who has required emergency treatment on
numerous occasions, she says, "Oh, yes! In fact the emergency room is
right on the corner." The clients may be healthy individuals reluctant
or unwilling to listen to the ear-shattering hullabaloo of ambulance
sirens racing past their driveway on an almost hourly basis. There's also
the possibility that the agent could incorrectly believe that bringing the
ER closer to home would increase the house's desirability, so instead of
saying, "The local hospital is half a mile south of the property," she says
"It's around the corner."

Assuming that clients are delighted by the proximity of a hospital, a
school, a bus or subway stop, or even a local park is a major error. It is
presumptuous because people have diverse needs and wants. An accom-
modation for one individual can be a nightmare for another and vice

versa. Assumptions are just another obstacle on the path to commission checks, a hindrance that causes agents to fall over their feet.

Once an agent has made a statement, it is impossible to retract it. The client has already formed an opinion about the property and most probably about the capability of the agent. There will unlikely be either a closing date or a referral name penciled on that REALTOR'S® calendar—she tripped over her own feet and will find it hard to get up.

Client History

If agents take the time to understand the needs and wants of their clients, inquire about the client's family and their requirements, then they will find the right properties to show and squander less time on "lemons" and those doomed-to-fail dramatic presentations. Bad agents are like a physician who fails to take a patient's medical history into account or ask about symptoms. Instead, learn the client's history. This allows agents to build a better reputation as a professional—a reputation based on excellent service and satisfying sales. Be thorough and put the client first. This differentiates an amateur and a mediocre agent from a qualified, profit-centered professional. The key to success is this *par excellence* status that determines an agent's worth and likewise the number and size of her commission checks.

3

Soft Sell for Hard Times

"My experience has shown me that the people who are exceptionally good in business aren't so because of what they know but because of their insatiable need to know more."

—Michael Gerber

Even top producers experience changes in income during fluctuating markets, but implementing a business system that works in conjunction with the prevailing trend allows agents to generate more leads—even in a less than sizzling market.

One thing I have learned is that a harder buyer's market is exciting for investors and scary for sellers. When currents shift, an agent's strategies must also swing to accommodate the change. I cannot emphasize enough the importance of keeping the right frame of mind. Agents in selling mode have to accept that their personal opinions are irrelevant—if not deal-busting.

Market Seesaw

The market is like a seesaw, sometimes up and sometimes down. Learn how to change position according to the swings and act in a way that is profitable. For instance, my advice regarding the sale of a property in a buyer's market would probably be: "Don't sell a thing. Hold onto it, even if it takes five or ten years for the market to swing around." Sounds like sound advice—but this approach doesn't work!

It fails because often people involved in the selling process are undergoing life changes. Perhaps they are relocating for employment or they are downsizing their home because circumstances have turned them from a family of four to empty nesters, or they may be moving from a starter house to a larger residence as their finances and children grow. Determine on which end of the seesaw your client sits.

People cannot put their lives on hold until the market swings into a more favorable position. Therefore, my opinion and that of every other REALTOR® is totally insignificant and better left unexpressed. It confuses, disturbs, and in the end may result in a client's struggle with buyer's remorse.

The All-Important Question: What Is Your Goal?

When addressing clients, the all-important question to ask is, "What is your goal?" In other words, try to learn what is best for your client at that very moment in time. Remember to always:

- Investigate the client's situation
- Ask about his future goals
- Try to find out what the client is looking for

- Discover what will work best for him

Taking the time to get answers will lead to more successful transactions.

Market Fluctuations—
Lingering Factor Versus Bidding War

In a fluctuating market, especially one dipping from hot to cool (or downright cold), agents are conditioned for multiple offers, easy deals, and transaction volume. Listing agents in particular are not required to work excessively or with enthusiasm in order to sell or market a property because there is no "lingering" factor—the houses or condos are selling after a day or two—and as a result of the bidding wars that arise in sizzling markets, properties sell well at list price or above. This upward trend equates to more substantial commission checks. As a result of this quick turnover, there is a continual surplus of new listings that attract REALTORS® like magnets.

When the bubble inflates, the selling becomes effortless, the earning abundant, and the roster of REALTORS® endless. However, when the market fluctuates and dips the number of agents actively working in the marketplace diminishes. They begin to dwindle because they are incapable of moving their transactions toward successful closings.

Selling Techniques

There are basically two types of selling techniques: the soft sell and the hard sell. From my perspective, the soft sell is always about service. It's not about applying the old "sweat hogs" Mike Ferry or Tommy Hopkins agent-training methods that spotlight overcoming objections, utilizing different systems, and responding to clients who say, "I'm not ready to sell, because the offer is too low," with a question like "how much is too low?" I consider this to be part of a canned strategy endorsed by too many REALTOR® educating programs.

This type of foundation-based training is rudimentary. It works for agents who are green behind the ears, have been in the business just a few years, and have closing calendars without any entries. I believe these introductory Real Estate 101 courses teach a method that falls short in a hard market because it is too much of a soft sell.

Anyone professing to know something about sales can typically see through this type of presentation style and will undoubtedly feel "sold." Instead, an agent looking for a winning strategy should sell the service and quality being provided. As a REALTOR® your mind-set should be programmed to reflect an attitude that asks how you can help meet your clients' need for selling this house or buying that investment property. This is a far cry from the canned rhetoric taught in most courses and unquestionably a soft sell.

When a sizzling easy-closing market changes course, agents find it almost impossible to rehab their sales strategies to fit the fluctuation. Then, properties linger for six months or longer. Inventory builds and gradually the supply begins to outweigh the demand. Nothing moves and the agent doesn't know how to survive in a commission check-free interim. Frustration bubbles up to fear and fear triggers a panic-motivated willingness to negotiate with intent to cut commissions in what may mistakenly seem to be a clever tactic to get more listings. This listing-buying, so to speak, is a poor financial scheme comparable to selling stocks in a bear market—something a smart investor would never consider.

Instead, what works more effectively is an approach based on educating the marketplace by shifting the business model from business that comes to you, to business that comes to you because you pursue it.

The Seminar Connection

An example of this strategy is the seminar concept. This is a way of gathering a wide range of people interested in learning more about real estate as a business venture. Through seminars, instead of "drizzle" marketing one house at a time, you are marketing to the mass population in your geographical area. This may sound somewhat confusing, but in reality it is rather simple. You are drawing potential prospects right to your door. They are coming to listen to your pitch because:

- They don't have, but *want* a qualified agent who will satisfy their needs in the best way possible.
- They are in search mode—ready to be persuaded into signing a listing or sales agreement with you.

In other words, this is your opportunity to flip good leads into clients who, if they are satisfied with your service, will refer family and friends.

The point of a seminar is to get the attention of prospective clients. When people sit in front of you, they seek you out for a specific motive—to have their questions answered and to gain information. Your task is to educate them and clear up their uncertainties. You can easily accomplish this by:

- Outlining, analyzing, and sharing market trends with your audience
- Being informative and able to answer questions about current trends in a specific marketplace
- Explaining the fluctuating time lines

- Telling them why listings today linger on the MLS whereas in the past, properties were snapped up immediately or shortly after profitable bidding wars

Have the Answers

Demonstrate your bravura as an agent:

- Let clients know that you are able and willing to go above and beyond. Help them understand the significance behind the statistic recording a 9.6-percent drop in the national average for home sales.
- Discuss how this percentage equates to Southern California, Boca Raton, Florida, or Denver, Colorado—in other words, different geographical areas with diverse economies.
- Explain how this relates to a prospective client and what influence it will have on her intention to invest.

Don't forget that a seller is interested in cashing in on his property appreciation option and is looking to get an investment profit when listing his house. Therefore, be prepared when a client asks:

- How can I get more money for my property in this bubble-bust market?
- How can I get a contract on my house in less time than it took to sell the house down the street?

The answers to these questions can differentiate between a signed listing agreement and a blank piece of paper!

As a real estate professional geared for success, your mind-set should be focused on providing potential prospects with valuable information in a cooling market. If you are knowledgeable and project self-confidence, clients will perceive you as a credible expert because you are the teacher and you are willing to give them clear-cut facts when most people are not.

Avoid Professional *Faux Pas*— Use a Client-Friendly Approach

The standard agent tactic is to put clients in a car and drive them around to preview a property—but only if they are convinced a sale is imminent. They don't pursue any line of questioning or information-accruing process. This professional *faux pas* leads to faulty judgments with respect to selecting properties that suit a client's needs. In return, prospects become exasperated by hopping from one unsuitable property to another. They become disenchanted with agents who don't allow them to ask questions or talk about what they are experiencing during the looking process. They loose faith in the agent's professional ability to "get it right." Once the bond of confidence wavers, the agent has lost a commission check and the referral part of her business plan.

Adopting an open and client-friendly approach encourages prospects to see value in the service that you provide. They appreciate the commitment to satisfying their needs and look upon the professional as a credible resource. Even though today may not be the day for a purchase or sales transaction, you have established a long-term relationship with the client.

Sharing knowledge breeds informed individuals—and informed individuals make more intelligent and satisfying decisions. As an agent, if you spend two or three days with people in a free or low-cost seminar, educating them and sharing the valuable fruits of your experience, you will have built a better rapport than another agent who spends an entire day chauffeuring people around the city to preview properties that turn out to be total misfits. With this educative strategy put into operation, you have successfully built a relationship that 98 percent of other agents are incapable of establishing. This becomes a soft sell because instead of selling, you are serving—giving the information clients need to help them make their own decisions based upon actual facts.

Hard Sell Versus Soft Sell

Many agents question how a hard sell differs from a soft sell. I differentiate between the two by defining a hard sell as a desperate approach that derives from using a lot of canned statements and systems. In essence, it is a canned *modus* of doing business.

An example of a statement canned would be a client saying, "I can't buy this house—the price is too high!" Most real estate training courses teach an objection-overcoming strategy based on asking, "It's too high by how much?" If the prospect responds that the house is $10,000 too high, the agent might say, "If you knew that $10,000 equated to a monthly payment of an additional $59.96, would that still be too much for you to carry?"

With this canned *modus,* the agent is removing the overpowering $10,000 figure and substituting it with a low monthly figure that is easier for the client to digest. An agent might go further, breaking it down into spending $14.99 a week and ask, "Is there anything you can give up to recuperate the $2.14 a day needed to override the excessive $10,000 price tag?"

What the agent has done is bring the objection down to a ridiculous level until it becomes practically nonexistent. At this point the client realizes that by substituting a morning *latte* enjoyed at a gourmet café with a steamed and brewed home version, he can afford to acquire his dream house.

This reduction to the absurd is the hard sell—a canned approach to closing a transaction. In essence it translates to figuring out how to take a client who says no and flip that no into acceptance.

The Tom Hopkins and Mike Ferry training courses are all hard-sell oriented. They teach the canned approach. Then it's the agent's responsibility to refine and polish the technique into a soft sell.

You can take the same situation involving a client who claims $10,000 is too much for him to carry and turn the initial hard approach into a soft sell by changing the content of your response. Take the same example, where the price is $10,000 above the client's bottom-line and ask him what it is about the property that he cannot afford.

In all likelihood the client will say that the mortgage payments are much too high. Once again, fall back on the same line of questioning and ask:

- How much is much too much?
- How much are those mortgage payments?

Perhaps he will say the extra $59.96 is too much. At this point alter your strategy and ask the client to tell you if the house somehow were not $59.96 over budget, if this would be *the* house. If the client says yes, demonstrate to him how to earn an extra $59.96 without doing anything except signing his name. Ask the client if at that point they would be agreeable to moving forward on the property.

Money in a Client's Hand

You put money in your clients' hands by sitting them down and explaining that they need to:

- Look at the tax deductions they claim at work. If they are claiming one exemption, there is a good possibility they can add another $13—maybe $14—to their income each week.

- Set up a meeting with their CPA or tax attorney and tell him they are planning to buy a house for a certain price with set mortgage payments in a specific amount. They should ask how they could save an extra $60 a month by combing through their finances to uncover possible deductions.

Once you educate clients, you not only show them how to change their deduction formula to accrue more money on a monthly basis, but also demonstrate the power they gain by using this strategy, whether they intend to purchase the original home or any other one.

Buying Power of Tax Deductions

The power of tax deductions lies in a simple rearrangement: a client is taking a noninvestment potential $60 every month that the government or her company would be holding for the client to pay taxes on, and she would be putting it into an appreciating asset. This asset would give the client:

- equity appreciation in the future; and
- a deduction at tax time that is far greater than the dollar amount she would have had without it.

Show clients what the numbers look like on paper and refer them to a tax specialist. This strategy is not to just sell them on it but to ask questions to get the necessary information and educate them regarding what they can and cannot do. You're not just going for the close and leaving them to figure out how they'll get it; you're working along with them, informing them of their options, and leading them to their final objective—the desired property.

Leads! Leads! Leads!

The more knowledge and time you are willing to give, the greater your commission potential will be. Satisfied clients will refer you, and your lead-generating ability will soar. A phenomenal agent knows that the name of the game is leads, leads, leads!

I have devised my own tried and proven lead-generating system (my financial freedom seminar system) that targets potential prospects by setting them in a situation in which they can meet me face to face, listen to what I have to say, and get answers to their questions. By developing this system, I became the number one agent for RE/MAX in the United States and currently hold the title for three consecutive years. I developed the system when I discovered that too many REALTORS® were incapable of dealing with me as an investor, and I wanted to be serviced by an agent who fully understood the real estate business, not just the paper passing aspect of presenting me with a contract to sign. I wanted them to be knowledgeable, savvy, and confident so that they would be aware of what I was doing and not be uncertain or fearful of the transactions. Often I would encounter difficulties when trying to get agents to work for me because they had stereotyped me as an investor, and in their minds investors wear you to the bone and empty your gas tank, making you work long and hard, and all for nothing in the end.

On the other hand, the truth has quite a different curb appeal. If you have a service approach and are offering an educational process, everyone becomes a client, and every single person can be sold a piece of property. That holds true if you're serving them properly. However, the sales technique has to be designed to work for the client—not for you, the agent.

Financial Freedom Seminar System

When I put my financial freedom seminar system together, I interviewed about 250 real estate professionals and polled them for their thoughts and opinions. All the agents told me they thought it was ridiculous. In their opinion, educating clients would not create a lead-generating vehicle. "It's just not going to work," they said, shaking their heads. Only one or two told me they thought it was a great idea, were certain it could work, and really liked the formula.

I didn't need solidarity. I knew I was onto a wining strategy—and it clearly works because I have achieved number one RE/MAX agent status for three years with closing commission checks totaling over $2 million. I built a system geared for success and based on:

- Treating people with respect
- Acknowledging their needs, wants and desires
- Educating them on available options that are both traditional and nontraditional in the real estate world

My financial freedom seminar system, a prospecting vehicle option that agents can choose to incorporate as part of their business model, is currently being franchised. REALTORS® or investors can purchase this franchise in their local area and enhance their business with a powerful lead-generating tool.

Most agents wonder how they can generate more leads. My answer is short and direct—the number one way you can grow leads is through a lead-generating system, such as providing information through inventive real estate seminars in which you learn how to teach the art of structuring creative transactions.

Creative Transactions

As an introduction, I define the mechanism of a creative transaction by what it is not—a 45-day escrow. It is instead:

- An 80-10-10 loan
- A lease option
- Taking a property subject to the existing financing
- Doing an all inclusive trust deed
- A lease option to purchase

I outline all of this information and feed it to REALTORS® so that they can grasp it and in turn be in a prime position to educate their clients regarding all the options available.

Seller Carryback Transaction. Most agents don't even know what a *seller carryback* is, and that it is beneficial to both parties in the transaction. During difficult economic times, you can have a property to sell and someone without sufficient funds for a down payment interested in buying that property. In a seller carryback transaction, the seller agrees to carry a second note and trust deed against the property, at a below-market interest rate, and forfeits all closing fees. In essence it is part of a seller financing strategy, in which the seller loans the buyer part of the seller's equity. The lender or mortgage company loans 90 percent of the purchase price whereas the seller loans 10 percent to complete the transaction. To make the deal even more creative, you can ask the seller to defer the payments on the second loan from 12 to 24 months or longer. This way, they're not paying a mortgage payment on that 10 percent. You can even ask the bank to carry 80 percent, the seller 20 percent, and have the seller defer the payment on that 20 percent. In addition you could ask the seller to credit you three percent of the closing fee, which can be used to make whatever improvement and repairs to the property that meet the loan guidelines. At the closing, if the lender approves it, you can walk away with three percent. On some loans you can actually leave the table with six percent.

Another example of an innovative and resourceful transaction is the short sale. I just recently put an offer on a property located in the Midwest. It was a short sale property and the seller was asking on the short sale $61,000. I wrote an offer to the bank for $48,000. The property received multiple offers. The seller was freaking out because she didn't know where her next destination would be. As part of my offer I said I would allow the current owner to remain on the premise for four months rent-free. It would take at least four months to foreclose on the property. She accepted my offer even though it was lower than the others were because the terms—not the price—was a factor in this transaction. More important than the dollars was the fact that she could remain for an additional four months. Part of the creative process is finding out what the buyer or seller needs and wants so you can satisfy them and in so doing get what you want.

Tough Market Sales Agreement. In a tough market, how does a seller get a signed sales agreement on his house faster than his neighbor does?

I've written over 400 offers in the past four months for investors who each have particular criteria to meet their requests. These investors are firm and refuse to budge; knowing that they can—and will—get their terms and conditions met.

When I first started writing these offers, the southern California market had just begun to fluctuate. The agents who received these offers held meetings to tell each other, "If you get this agent's offer, don't give it to your seller. It's a ridiculous offer and we don't want to work with it." These agents were thinking only of their diminished commission checks and personal feelings about presenting a low offer. Yet they failed to consider that their decision not to present the offer was infringing upon the law.

One agent phoned me to say that he had put my offer right in the trash can because he had no intention of presenting it to the seller. The offer in question was a full-price offer asking for a 6-percent credit back at closing and a 10-percent seller carry.

The property was listed for $800,000 and taking off six percent as a credit equated to $48,000. The agent told me that under no circumstances would his seller agree to be out 16 percent! When I asked how the seller would be out 16 percent, he responded that they were giving 10 percent because they were providing the financing. I told him it was a loan and they would be making interest on it. It was clear that my explanation of the rather simple process was beyond his comprehension. Apparently he was clueless.

I volunteered to walk him through the process.

"Well then he's still giving six percent," he said interrupting my train of thought. "So it means that out of $800,000, $80,000 is gone. This makes the seller's net $672,000 before commissions are paid."

I told him he was correct. The seller still has the $80,000—he just gets it at a later date. The agent let out a sigh and told me the client would get it if the buyers didn't default. He was missing the point: Even in a worse case scenario prior to commissions and closing fees the net would be $672,000.

I thought I had actually gotten through to him so I was somewhat surprised to hear him say that this was the most pathetic offer he had ever seen—and that it was a huge disgrace to the entire real estate community. I told him I was sorry he felt that way but if he was open for discussion, I wanted to take the opportunity to explain why the offer had been written in that manner.

Once again his irritated mood and the aggressive way in which he snapped at me, shouting that nothing I could do or say would change his opinion about the transaction surprised me. Before I could respond, he rudely hung up on me.

Dealing with the Uneducated Agent

Believe it or not, this was not an uncommon call regarding the 400 offers I had written. I received 100 similar phone calls and about 200 others from agents who just did not understand and were not willing to give me a chance to explain.

Not being one to stay in the background, I put together an email video message that went through the offers in order to educate the agents who were upset with me simply because they did not understand the workings of the process. When you opened the video message, I would pop up, speak to them in a video, and explain the offer. After my video presentation, many of the agents phoned me asking if I could walk them through the process because they were having difficulty understanding it. This got me thinking: perhaps there was a faster way to do this in which the agents could present their offers without calling me to go over what I had just told them. I worked on more email video messages to walk agents through the various scenarios of different, more creative transactions. It worked out quite nicely.

Going back to the $800,000 property: to this day it's still on the market, its price has been reduced five times, and the current list price is $650,000. Had my offer been accepted, the seller would have sold the property, netted the $672,000, taken a chance on a second of $80,000, and moved on, but because the agent didn't believe my argument and refused to present it to the seller, the seller never received my offer. This is where agents step all over themselves by not letting the clients make the decisions.

I tracked every one of the 400 offers I put out just to see how many that refused the offer had gone through multiple price reductions. Four months after my offers, 80 percent have come back to me and asked if my client was still interested—and I still have people calling. They were unable to transition from a sizzling market to a cool market. Foolishly and mistakenly, they believed that they were still in a hot market, so they were arrogant, uneducated, and unwilling to deal.

Always Present Offers

Agents will often tell me they are expecting multiple offers, and therefore they are going to wait before presenting the first one that comes in. This is a bad strategy because where does it say, for instance, in the California Association of REALTORS® ethical guidelines that you cannot present all offers when you have five others? It says "present all offers in a timely manner." Time is of the essence in getting a signed sales agreement.

Whether it's a sizzling or cool market:

- Business is business
- Present your offers
- Give your clients a chance to make a decision
- Get educated
- Learn how to put together creative deals
- Don't dismiss an offer because it is inventive; if you think it's ridiculous and want to enjoy a good laugh on a personal level, do it—but then after the chuckle, figure out a strategy that will get you a commission check
- Counter an offer—never cancel a transaction; let the other side make that decision

An agent phoned me once complaining because we were presenting the 15th counteroffer. I asked him if his intention was to stop the process saying, "Your client keeps countering, and so does mine. So what if we have fifteen offers? We can have one hundred as far as far as I'm concerned!"

Unsatisfied with my response, he decided to talk about it. He wanted to discuss cleaning it all up and possibly putting in one final offer.

I was not in favor of discussing any strategies with him because I felt I was not in charge of that decision. Whenever a client wants to counter, let her counter. If in the end you want to clean it up in an escrow instruction then by all means go ahead.

Commission Checks in a Market Spin

What many agents fail to comprehend is that the main success factors in a shifting market are to be able to quickly identify the change, adapt to the fluctuation as quickly as possible, and always do good business regardless of your personal opinion. In a slow market the best way to spot the market change the moment it happens and make the transition is always to work as if you're in a difficult market.

Adopting this winning mind-set will guarantee you a full closing calendar and a surplus of commission checks to deposit!

4

Courage to Build
the Life You Deserve

"Life shrinks or expands in proportion to one's courage."

—Anais Nin

If you have the courage to explore creative options and the passion to educate clients, you will be stacking your commission checks like bricks and building the lifestyle you want and deserve. It takes an enterprising spirit and self-confidence based on knowledge and information to put together—sometimes in unconventional ways—transactions that will give your clients the opportunity to weigh their options and make their own decisions.

Deleting Old-School Uncreative Strategies

Many times REALTORS® fall into the habit of listening to other agents discuss their methods and strategies instead of asking themselves:

- How would I handle this scenario?
- How would I present this option for structuring, accepting, or countering an offer?

They listen to everyone else and go with the flow. This is the old-school way of doing real estate—and I define old school as a method that doesn't include seller carrybacks or where the interest rate should always be anchored at eight percent. In other words, the old-school way is comprised of strategies that are rather uncreative.

As mentioned in a previous chapter, most real estate companies don't provide new agents with good training. Consequently they fall back on the old way of doing things. Yet to be a good and profitable agent with a stack of commission checks to deposit, you absolutely cannot think like the masses. You don't want mediocre statistics—you want to do extraordinary business.

To increase your profit potential, it is necessary to look at creative options and decide what you would do in a given transaction. It takes courage to step out. It takes guts to make your own decisions regardless of the popular opinion—especially when you are nervous and afraid and questioning if a certain option will lead to a closing or a walk away.

Agent Conditioning

When an offer is presented, many agents feel uncertain if it asks for a seller credit plus a seller carryback in addition to all sorts of concessions. Often a strong agent representing the other side of the transaction comes back with a sassy "What are you crazy? There's no way we'll make those concessions—put together a different offer!" The result is that the agent shuts down, thinking he can't ask for seller credit or carryback simply because the other agent seemed offended. Basically the agent has conditioned himself for failure.

Agents facing this situation are afraid to present an offer because others have told them it's not a good one. They base their final decision on another agent's judgment call. It takes a huge amount of courage to decide how you will represent the client. In these circumstances, think of Eleanor Roosevelt, who said, "You gain strength, courage, and confidence by every experience in which you really stop to look fear in the face. You must do the thing which you think you cannot do."

Believe in Your Beliefs

In my office, I ask agents to consider what their beliefs dictate to them about the right thing to do. Once they have the answer, I encourage them to step up to it, and more importantly act on it when preparing a transaction on behalf of a client.

This is why and where some agents remain mediocre and others excel to become top performers. The big achievers are not afraid to set out and try something new to close a deal. They are neither scared nor hesitant to consider a tactic even if it's not from an old-school method of business that has proven merits.

I have an agent working with me now who has held a license and been in the business for almost 20 years. We recently traveled to the Virgin Islands to make an offer on a property. I told her to watch how I structured the offer and worked through the deal.

The property was priced at $5.9 million. I offered $3.4 million completely furnished, including the seller's boat. The selling agent looked at the offer and told me it was ridiculous. She instructed us to look at all the comparables. In her opinion, the lowest acceptable offer would be approximately 15 percent below the asking price. I told her that as far as I was concerned, my offer was perfectly appropriate.

The selling agent contacted me again, certain I would consider raising my offer to get the property. I caught her off guard when I told her that I initially intended to offer less than my current offer but had decided to stick with my last offer. I devised my strategy based on the idea that although the comparables were a verified factor, I didn't personally believe the property was worth more. Therefore, I set the value at $3.4 million for the house, the furniture, and the boat.

The agent who had accompanied me to the Virgin Islands told me she thought I was just as nutty as the other agent thought I was. I gave her a let's-wait-and-see shrug. Keeping my offer intact, I returned to the United States. Shortly thereafter I received an email from the seller asking if he could speak with me directly. He had read my name on the offer, found my website, and tracked me down. He phoned me and we put a deal together with an offer at $3.6 million including, as stated in my original offer, property, furniture, and boat. It was a beautiful transaction. Had I listened to the seller's agent and subtracted 15 percent from the $5.9 million asking price, I would have paid much more than the $3.6 million—and had I not known better maybe I would have actually believed I was both ridiculous and nuts!

It took about three and a half months of negotiations to put the deal together. Nevertheless, had I listened to the listing agent instead of following my own intuition, I would have based my offer on comparables as an alternative to establishing my own value and would have definitely overpaid for the property according to my personal appraisal.

Boundless Strategies

Too often people determine a property's worth by a mechanism called market value. In my opinion, there are two categories of value:

- Market value based on comparative market analysis
- Market value calculated by my personal property analysis and appraisal—in other words, what I'm willing to pay

This doesn't mean that the market value isn't substantiated. It just means that in my opinion I should not pay that much for a property because my reason for acquiring it—how I intend to use it—does not warrant a market value price.

An agent who can step away from the market value conditioning norm and its give-or-take-10-percent attitudes will be able to help clients make money and increase her own chances to earn money as a wise investor. When you see this results-oriented concept in action, and start to see your new approach bring more deals to the closing table, you will feel excited and motivated to put together more creative transactions.

The RE/MAX agent who had accompanied me to the Virgin Islands was amazed when I closed the deal for $3.6 million with all my conditions honored. "Oh, my God" she said. "That's incredible!"

What was exceedingly more inconceivable to me was that after her 18-year career as a REALTOR®, this agent found my reasoning, strategy, and outcome to be ridiculous. With almost two decades of experience as a REALTOR®, she should be writing all sorts of creative deals—low offers, high offers. I was certain she would adopt a strategy without boundaries and try everything and anything, fully acknowledging that an agent can't always predict what a seller will accept in a given moment.

Typically a REALTOR® represents the seller, therefore as listing agent his objective is to get if not list price, the highest price for the client. However, if you're the buyer, you represent yourself, not the seller, so it makes sense to close the deal, getting the best possible price.

Thinking Outside the Box

Agents should take the time to look at transactions from the buyer's and seller's perspectives. They should learn to think outside the box. Step into the purchaser's role and question what they would rather do—pay $5.9 million or $3.6 million for the property of interest? The answer is undoubtedly clear. The point is, if they prefer to pay $3.6 million, why do they assume their client would be willing to pay $5.9 million?

In 2006, I sent one of my agents to Aspen, Colorado, with 15 referrals—at the time, the Aspen market was red hot. In our offers we asked the seller to credit some money for closing costs and do seller carrybacks.

The agent flew to Aspen and phoned me to announce he had talked to my broker and was told we shouldn't do this because the broker felt the offers were way too low and we should bump them up. The broker said the market is so hot that the low offers were painfully embarrassing.

Sensing another wave of opposition, I countered telling the broker he had to be joking. I questioned his intention not to present the offers, but he was deadset against it. Defending his refusal, he complained that he would be laughed at and ridiculed if he ever dared present the offers.

Never accepting the mistake of in-the-box conventional thinking, I went on title, found the names of the owners, and phoned them directly. When I had them on the line I presented myself to each one as a licensed REALTOR® in the State of California. I mentioned that although I was licensed to sell in Colorado, I had a client who was interested in acquiring their property under the following terms and conditions. Taking it further I informed them I was having difficulties getting an agent to present the offers because they all seem to find it embarrassing.

I paused then continued asking them to tell me if they thought it was way out of place. I emphasized, however, that if I were the property owner, I would want to see every offer made before I would make my decision whether to accept or refuse.

Six out of the 15 offers I presented met with a favorable response and proceeded to the closing table. In this case, by refusing to stand on his own two feet, my agent forfeited six escrows because he was unwilling to submit the offers and try to put the transaction together. He walked away without even having the courage to try! This is definitely not a formula for success.

Rehabbing the Norm

Having the courage to create the life you deserve is about being brave enough to break away from the norm. It's having the courage to operate under an "expectancy" rule. This means:

- Believing that you're entitled to find good properties at great value that you can flip, sell, or own
- Thinking that sellers are at liberty to get the most money—even the listing price—for their property

The objective is to find sellers who are willing to give you the price you believe the property is worth. This is a win-win situation.

The only way agents can have hordes of commissions checks to deposit that add up to over $500,000 is by changing their mind-set from doing what everyone else does to what everyone else doesn't do!

Actually it's the same principle as in successful marketing—you find a unique selling proposition and you put it to use. As an agent, you must do likewise. For me the unique spot is the realization that some agents consider investors nutty and don't want to work with them. I always heard in real estate that "buyers are liars and looky loos"; they'll tell you what they want, and then buy something totally different.

Stepping Up to the Plate

I always tell agents to step up to the plate—learn how to write a creative offer and have the courage to present it. When a buyer tries to dictate how an offer should be written, don't get choked up, chuckle over it, or roll your eyes as if you're in preseizure mode. Instead treat them with the utmost professionalism, write the best offer possible, and present it to the other agent.

The underlying objective is to get the clients into the negotiation process as soon as possible. Until an offer hits the seller's hand, everyone is clueless about what the buyer will or will not do. However once it hits, the game has begun! It's time to roll with the negotiations.

It takes a lot of courage to present an offer that you think someone will ridicule, but if you don't attribute a laughable quality to it in your mind, if you visualize its final outcome as positive, and if you get the buyer and seller to give a little, then who cares how the offer was first received? The important element is that the deal closed and you have a commission check to deposit. What you should care about is the result—not the fact that the initial offer was $2 million below list price—or that someone thought you were nuts. The commission justifies taking the chance and presenting the offer.

Too often for their own good, agents are looking for a first offer-closing deal. That means it's up to you to find the best deal for you and:

- write it,
- present it, and
- close it.

Of course, it doesn't usually work that way. You can't always design the transaction according to an unfeasible proposal of perfection.

For example, let's say that you call an agent for showing instructions on her listed property and instead of accommodating you, she makes it difficult. She is arrogant, dismissive, and angry. Obviously you will decide not to show her listing. Instead you will search for others that meet your client's requirements and are listed with cooperative professional agents who are looking for commission checks, not a sounding board to release pent-up emotions. Because of the unaccommodating agent, a seller lost a potential deal and the seller's and buyer's agents forfeited commission checks. Had the listing broker been more available and involved, the property would have had more showings, which would have increased the potential for a sale.

Weeks later you receive a phone call. "You called for showing instructions," the disgruntled REALTOR® shouts. "You said you were going to show my property—so why didn't you show it?" There is only one logical response: to say that you called for showing instructions, but the agent really didn't make it all that pleasant because when you called to inform her you had a client who wanted to preview the property, her reaction sent up a red flag. Your first impression was that she was disgruntled and rather disturbed by your request and had little if any interest in being accommodating. Therefore you didn't want to be in an escrow with her.

Avoiding the Cement Ceiling

Agents have the power of the MLS to research, find, and show clients available properties. The surplus and easy access allows for selectivity. REALTORS® will show properties if they feel the listing agents are cooperative. Consequently a mind-set built on action, client/agent satisfaction, and accomplishment is the foundation for successfully showing and closing properties. Anything less is an invitation for disaster.

Agents and clients tend to work well with people who are professional and willing to move toward a win-win scenario—getting into escrow. Based on their behavior, many agents get what they deserve, be it positive or negative. In my lengthy career in real estate I have found that some agents are stubborn and set in their old-school ways of doing business. They feel as if they are the supreme authority and govern the business. Their attitude is "my way or no way." Usually these REALTORS® are top-producers but belong to a category that I believe is stagnant. They hit a cement ceiling and fly no higher, earning $250,000 a year every single year. You can pat them on the back for being top-producers, but ask them to break their own record and earn $251,000, and they go into a spin because they just don't know how to increase their business. They settle comfortably into a familiar pattern and are incapable of change, remaining stuck at a certain level and never moving forward.

Positive affirmations and the ability to pump yourself up to be different, to excel, and to go one step beyond will ensure your success. If you truly believe you deserve it, and if you want and will it, then you will get it. However, if you feel you're unworthy, incapable, and undeserving, so shall you be.

Ruiz's Four Agreements

I like to refer to theories of Don Miguel Ángel Ruiz, a Mexican-born physician and surgeon. About 10 years ago, he wrote *The Four Agreements,* a book in which he discusses a personal disengagement from our agreements and beliefs both involving ourselves and others. He explains that the very mind-set by which we govern our lives often builds crippling boundaries. Consequently we find ourselves unhappy, dissatisfied, and unsuccessful in achieving our goals. Ruiz's journey is a pursuit for personal integrity, self-love, and harmony within.

I agree wholeheartedly with his *Four Agreements,* which I applied to my own life, both professional and personal. The agreements are:

- Be impeccable with your word.
- Don't take anything personally.
- Don't make assumptions.
- Always do your best.

I truly believe that if real estate agents could adopt these agreements, they wouldn't take personally the offers presented and the reactions that result. Instead, they would accept every offer as business—an opportunity to get the ball rolling, the dialogue happening, and the communication and negotiations started.

If they seriously considered adapting Ruiz's Agreements, REALTORS® would learn it is wise not to assume an outcome. In other words, they would not enter the transaction with a preconceived idea of how the buyers and sellers will act and react. This mind-set serves only to condition the key players against negotiating and condemns the deal before it even takes off. In addition, of course adopting a work ethic that calls for doing your absolute best encourages agents to work in the best interest of their clients, present all the offers, and be as professional as possible to instill confidence.

Being impeccable to your word is another important rule for achieving success. This means that you should never make promises you are unable or unwilling to fulfill. Reliability is not an easy trait to achieve. It can be a tear-down asset with just one slip up. A disappointed client is unlikely to do business with an agent who doesn't carry through on her word.

Many times I have overhead agents on the phone telling clients, "I'll take care of that for you. Don't worry you'll have all the docs in 30 minutes." Then they go off with another client to show property, or head out to lunch with a colleague, completely forgetting the promises they made just moments earlier.

On other occasions I have heard REALTORS® assure their clients saying, "I'm going to present the offer right now," then hang up, get on the phone with the listing agents and say, "I know this is a stupid offer but I'm obligated to present it!" This type of integrity deficiency doesn't help anyone. This loser's strategy is the double-sided conversation. The client is told one thing and the other agent another (often the complete opposite). This is not professionalism.

When I think about professionalism in business, I always focus on Don Miguel Ruiz's book. It is a good guide offering simple but valuable advice all linked to his four agreements. It shows people how to get what they deserve and design the manner in which they will go about achieving it.

If you structure your business model according to the *Four Agreements,* you will know that you are conducting yourself in the most professional way possible, and that you are doing good business. As a result you are more in harmony with the transaction, and you are working with positive energy and prohibiting negativity from getting the upper hand.

If you tell a client something and then somersault the entire conversation when speaking to someone else, you're not acting with integrity. In this scenario you don't even have a fighting chance for achieving the goals and objectives you want, because you have set yourself up for failure before you even get started. Instead, have the courage to set your self up for success and follow through on what it takes to achieve.

The Courage to Know What You Want

Courage is necessary not only to build the life you deserve, but also to assess if you really want to lead a particular lifestyle. People say they want money. They dream about an affluent lifestyle; they talk about it and do what they believe needs to be done in order to achieve it. Yet, what they fail to admit to themselves is that deep down they are afraid of the responsibility associated with attaining their goal.

I don't think that people always understand what they are getting themselves into. Often in focusing on the outcome, they seem to sidestep the responsibility factor. I have had many experiences with individuals who wanted to become wealthy, yet once the objective was achieved they just couldn't handle all the ramifications because often they didn't take the time to comprehend what they were getting themselves into.

Whenever I hear someone in the office say, "I want to be a top producer. I want to be a number one agent." I look around the office at the 350 REALTORS® who work there and try to discover who held the top honor last year. Once I know who the agent is, I try to find out how many transactions he executed during the previous year, and how many commissions he closed in dollar amounts. When I'm quoted a figure such as $700,000, I find it interesting to note how this number is perceived. Depending upon your consciousness $700,000 either seems minimal, unachievable, or any spectrum in between.

Subtle Persuasion

When your consciousness latches on to the reality of what it means to be a top agent—what it actually takes in hard work and commitment—you often realize you really don't want to be a top agent. If you ask yourself why, you might tell yourself that you just can't do what it takes. In essence you have already convinced yourself it's not what you want. It's subtle persuasion. You simply talked yourself right out of it.

In defining your wants and needs, the courage factor again comes into play. It takes a lot of courage to decide what you truly do and don't want for your life. Once this is accomplished, however, you set yourself in a position to achieve the goals you really desire and you are able to stay clear of the ones that were not meant to be yours in the first place.

Here is a prime example of this mechanism. Not long ago, one of my business partners, a real estate professional for two decades, announced she was resigning. Surprised by her decision, I told her, "This is really out of the blue!"

She admitted I was right but justified her decision by telling me she realized it was too much work for her. She wanted the opportunity to walk away and she appreciated the possibility of using the heavy work-load as her excuse. Apparently she loved real estate, but she just didn't want to work that hard. Open and genuine, she certainly understood what she was willing to do and not do to satisfy her needs and by leaving she acted upon her decision.

In another conversation, she confided in me that she doubted her ability to succeed because she was doing too much at once.

Consequently she was happier and liked it better when she excelled at one thing—being a top agent. In effect she was the top agent; a title she shared with being the only REALTOR® in her own company. It was kind of humorous but it demonstrated she had the talent and ability to earn an excellent income. However, when it came down to seizing a business opportunity, she realized it was not what she truly wanted. Yet it took her almost 18 months to arrive at this conclusion and to discover that this was not how she envisioned her professional life. She was not willing to take on a heavy travel schedule and other obligations that were not required in her life as an agent. Therefore, all the financial success meant nothing to her because she regarded the responsibility as unworthy of the result.

In living this experience with her, I began to reflect back on all the REALTORS® I had encountered at our annual meetings and awards dinners. I noticed that the same agents are given awards every year. To myself I said, "Maybe all those agents who never reach the podium don't want to." Maybe it's just not in their mind-set to excel, and those who do get the awards are not guaranteed the same success in the future. One wrong attitude, one doubted affirmation, and it's another end result.

There is no certainty. There is, however, a lot of courage involved in deciding what you want and don't want. Once you arrive at a conclusion, and figure out what is best for you at a specific moment in time, you are free to head in a clear direction and achieve your goal quicker by:

- Setting your intention
- Being responsible for working toward achieving it
- Assuming the responsibility such a goal requires

Real Estate Spirituality

My whole belief system is based on the philosophy that everything has a very strong spiritual undertone. I believe that what I put into the universe by setting my intention, I will receive from the universe. If you realize and accept this as a valid concept, setting and achieving objectives become easier—the journey to your destination appears shorter. You will see that there are less detours and obstacles along the way. It also becomes more pleasant because you are not met with conflict.

Courage is also about understanding the nature and scope of resistance and opposition, and allowing it to pass. For example, when a transaction falls short do you ever think that maybe it's not meant to be?

Some agents work themselves into a frantic dither as the closing date approaches, whereas others walk through the waiting period calm and collected, confident the outcome of the deal will be positive. Some panic, threaten, and get all wound up in a frenzy. Still others enjoy every moment of the process maintaining a serene composure.

Usually when a property fails to close, months pass and when you investigate who was supposed to buy it, why they didn't close, and what they acquired instead, most probably you will realize the final outcome was a much better solution than what they were originally fighting to get.

Sometimes agents need to learn how to let go when the buyers and sellers have let go. Usually buyers and sellers know intuitively when it's not the right situation or when it's over with. If agents continue to hold on and force the transaction just to walk off with a commission check, it creates negativity. This in turn pushes the deal further away in addition to creating a nasty taste in everyone's mouth.

Know When It's Over

It takes a lot of courage to accept that a deal is falling through. If the client says it's over—it's over. Let it go. You still have the client to work with. Haggling and stubborn persistence won't put a check in your hand. It will cause you to lose a client.

Just because one transaction was soured doesn't mean the client isn't interested in pursuing other property options. A lot of agents forfeit their clients because they continue to hang on when it's so apparent that the deal is dead.

Be courageous—let go and let your client be at choice. Offer optimum service and be gracious with your client. Tell them, "You are at liberty to go anywhere and you're free to work with whomever you like. What I'm going to do is help you regardless of whom you work with or where you go. This is just what I do. My life is about service. The more I serve you, the more you are encouraged and motivated to serve, and the more I get served in return in one way or another. This is my commitment to doing my best for you."

Commitment

Besides courage, commitment plays a major role in obtaining positive outcomes. What drives me really crazy is witnessing people getting within an inch of achieving their goals and then running out of steam, a phenomenon also known as quitting! They just can't seem to go the extra mile.

Many agents ask me to define commitment in the real estate business. Commitment for a REALTOR® equates to the mantra: "I'm in the business to help you, whether you buy from me or you don't," because the underlying mentality is "I'm in this business for the long run. I recognize that you could be my client five years from now because I served you well today and I served you prioritizing your needs without any display of disappointment for not earning a commission check."

Having the courage to commit to the lifestyle you deserve is also about building a successful business. Don't forget that real estate is a business that you build bit by bit for the long run. It is a business based on referrals and repeat clients.

Nothing happens until you are ready to commit, and once you are committed there is nothing that can't happen.

5

Hot Market Sales Versus Cold Market Sales

"Every day, you'll have opportunities to take chances and to work outside your safety net. Sure, it's a lot easier to stay in your comfort zone...in my case, business suits and real estate...but sometimes you have to take risks. When the risks pay off, that's when you reap the biggest rewards."

—Donald Trump

Selling in a fast-paced hot market differs from selling in a sluggish soft market. When the market shifts, you need to be savvy and informed. These are the times that separate the dilettante, temporary agents from the powerhouse professionals. Skilled REALTORS® do not falter in a sluggish soft market because they have an understanding of the concepts needed to put deals together. The temporary agent hides failure and a commission deficit behind a soft market alibi, whereas seasoned professionals spot the changing market and adapt their business strategies accordingly. As a result of their flexibility in technique and approach, they earn commission checks.

I recently concluded a class for a group of real estate agents at the Learning Annex. The topic I covered was bubble-proof strategies for REALTORS®. The room was filled with my favorite audience: skeptical seasoned REALTORS® and brand new "afraid to do anything" agents.

As I finished telling the class that a REALTOR'S® opinion does not matter and is best left unexpressed, one of the students asked, "How do I answer my clients when they ask me if this is a good market to buy in?" My response: Only the opinions of the buyers and sellers are relevant in a transaction.

The student assured me that she understood what I had said but insisted in her pursuit to find another answer—surely there is a secret to determining a good buyer's market, she assumed. On one hand I was amused by her persistence but frustrated by the fact that she just didn't get it.

Seeing my uneasiness, she rephrased her question: "What if the clients just want my expertise?" I asked her if she thought real estate was a good investment. When she nodded her head in agreement, I asked if she believed that real estate appreciates or depreciates in value. She said "appreciates." Then I asked if she thought this was a good market. We were in the best buyer's market ever, she declared, so I asked her why she made that assumption.

She took a deep breath and told me that in her experience, buyers will not buy unless they can get the property for what they want to pay. In addition, all the sellers have to agree.

I had to admit that even though she didn't quite understand my point about remaining objective and keeping all personal opinions out of it, this time, she was right.

Distinguishing Between Hard and Soft Markets

Distinguishing between a hard and soft market is not about following the newspapers, radio, and television newscasters who broadcast and expound upon the changing markets and fluctuating interest rates. Of course these factors should be considered, but from an intuitive and fact-based perspective it's wise to investigate the marketplace. Talk to other REALTORS® and see what other sellers are accepting. Discover what kind of transactions are moving toward closings.

Sitting Time and Price Reduction

When properties have a longer "sitting" time, and sellers are willing to carryback second mortgages, it is indicative of a changing market. You can also look at the terms sellers are agreeing to, and the trend toward price reduction. If you drive down the street or read the real estate ads and notice "price reduced" advertising, it is pretty obvious that the sizzle has cooled and you're slipping into a soft market.

On the other hand, if you see just one agent with a "price reduced" ad that is certainly not a valid indicator of a market fluctuation. It is instead, an example of a REALTOR® not knowing how to price a property properly and having to enter a correction.

Hard and Soft Market Strategies

I think the biggest difference between a hard and soft market depends on:

- The capability of agents to understand how to structure offers
- The ability to learn how to deal with negotiations from a listing agent's perspective

There are valid resources for REALTORS® to consult when trying to set a business model for a specific market trend. One important factor is to get accurate financial data regarding interest rates in order to be able to offer clients the best financing options. When interest rates rise, the market softens, and when rates dip, the market flips to favor buyers.

Agents should learn how to structure better transactions in order to successfully deal in a softer market. Most people enter the real estate profession when the markets are hot. They see how much money agents are making, get a license, and jump right in.

Sure money is easily made in a sizzling market because multiple offers roll in. However, as soon as the tide slows and it becomes evident that it takes strategy and work to collect commission checks, agents realize how limited they are and how little they know about closing a deal in a soft market.

Top producing agents prepare for fluctuating market trends. They understand it is important to set up a business model that includes revenues streams, especially in anticipation of a changing tide.

Setting Up a Business Model

In setting up a business model, there are several steps to follow:
- First, have a vision for the business. This involves setting objectives and planning the means to attainment.
- Next, it is important to identify the target market.
- Once this has been established it is essential to decide what strategy you will utilize to reach this specific market.

Decide what form of marketing you will use—"door-knocking" strategies, telemarketing, direct mail, seminar. Determine also whether you will utilize one specific tool or an adaptation of many diverse forms.

Once you have decided on your marketing strategy, it is essential to implement time-management concepts. This involves devising a schedule regarding when you will perform each of the tasks in your plan, and how you will measure the validity of each task—also known as the success factor.

Many people jump in and invest money in massive advertising campaigns. They send out flyers, take out ads in newspapers and REALTOR® periodicals, design glossy eye-catching brochures, postcards, and newsletters, and rent a bench or space on the side of a public transportation vehicle and plaster it with their name and number. In a word they spend big bucks on what I call "Madison Avenue" advertising on Main Street, USA. However, the question I ask is—does this expensive marketing pay off? Surprisingly many agents respond, "I don't know."

Tracking Marketing Strategies

When I see REALTORS® using many of these marketing tools, I know immediately that some of them who shelled out money for blitz advertising have no plan. I often see the same agents' ads in four or five publications. This tells me they have no way of tracking who responds as a result of which ad.

They can't track their responses because they use the same telephone number on all their advertising. Every ad reads "call my cell phone!" Consequently they can't distinguish a successful marketing strategy from a campaign that wastes money and time.

In my seminars, I recommend that in all forms of marketing, agents keep a log to track which tool is a good marketing investment—by that

I mean brings in money. Agents can identify leads through the utilization of separate telephone extensions or a 1-800 call-capture system in which it is feasible to catch the caller's info. In this way you can track how many individuals phoned from the newspaper ads and how many from brochures or rent-a-bench advertisements. Once the best tool is identified, it is wise to eliminate the least efficient, and put your money on a vehicle that brings in valuable leads—clients that end up at the closing table.

Tracking allows for smart marketing strategies. No one would think of investing in the stock market without checking to see what kind of return a stock is earning. The same is true with marketing—it is essential to monitor the success rate of a particular marketing strategy.

Both hot and soft markets warrant business systems. Of course they should be tweaked depending on current trends, but if you have a strong business system in place you can pretty much withstand any market, by merely learning how to make the few minor adjustments to comply with a hot, cold, or dead market.

After identifying the target market, pinpointing the types of advertising, and learning how to supervise the marketing process, it is essential to track your own success rate by calculating how many calls you receive from a specific ad. Once you have the number of callers you can determine how many of those individuals you were able to set appointments with. If 10 people responded to your ad, and five agreed to an appointment, you have a 50-percent call-in conversion ratio. Then take it a step further. Out of the five who came into the office, calculate how many resulted in a closing. If you close two and half deals, once again you have a 50-percent conversion ratio from appointment to sale.

Monitoring Success

As an agent, real estate is your business and it should be treated as such. Once you have tracked your marketing dollars, it is opportune to monitor your personal success. This allows you to identify your own strengths and failings. For instance, a 50-percent closing rate is a pretty decent result, but if you discover that from the 100 phone calls you receive, you were only able to set one appointment, then it's time to analyze your business model. The advertising brings in the calls, but you are incapable of moving them further because even though your marketing works, you need to rehab your business strategy.

The Art of Profitable Strategizing

I had a relatively new agent in my office. Joe was 25, licensed, and had been doing real estate for a couple of years. He was quite sure of himself. When I asked him to define the type of salesperson he was, I got a quick and direct: "I'm incredible. I close 90 percent of the people I deal with."

The surprising factor was not his self-assured response; but that he left real estate not long after he got into it because he couldn't sell enough in one of the hottest markets in the history of California real estate! Apparently he was overevaluating his own success quotient and not selling as much as he wanted me to believe.

Disappointed by his not-up-to-par closing statistics, he decided to become a loan officer, and went to work for a loan company that generated leads for him. Several months later he bragged to me that he was the top person in the company with the highest sales figures to his credit. In fact he boasted he was in line to become a net branch of the organization. This new position would enable him to originate loans in multiple states.

I congratulated him and asked about his business plan—a valid consideration in my opinion. He told me he was going to bring in a few people and set up his own loan company.

Then he got to the meat of the question. Joe told me his strategy involved hiring all the REALTORS® who had left real estate because they were unable to sell. They were all licensed and eager to become loan officers. It all sounded good, because according to Joe, he had no problems whatsoever; no issues with his lead to closing ratios, and he brought all his transactions to a profitable outcome.

I listened in silence to his boasting before making a comment. I told him I was a bit perplexed because he said he had no problems, yet if he was unable to make it as a REALTOR® in one of the hottest markets in history why did he think the situation would be different with loans?

His answer came quickly. Prospecting was always hard for him he told me, but this company gives him the leads. As a result he closes every day. Still curious to pursue his line of thinking, I asked him how many leads he is passed every day.

My question seemed to fall on deaf ears for a few brief moments until he admitted that he was absolutely guaranteed one a day.

I couldn't believe he was actually sitting at his desk waiting for one lead a day. As a loan officer, he could spend eight hours away from his office meeting 30 new agents who are doing business and each of them could send him one lead a day.

Intrigued, I took it further. I asked how many phone calls he made to get leads. Much as I expected, he responded that he made a ton of calls, but when I asked him to show me the phone log, he blurted out rather defensively, as if I was being unfair or accusatory, that he didn't write them down.

At this point I told him it really wasn't valid to refer to himself as wildly successful when he did not track his results while struggling financially. There is one thing I know with certainty—your bank account reflects the amount of effort you put into something, whether it be intellectual energy or hard labor. Therefore, if the numbers in your bank account are not exactly thrilling, it's more than likely because you failed to put together a business strategy that would add up to those figures.

Gutting Goals

One of the things I like to recommend to agents is a backing out of your goals technique. In other words: rehab your original objectives. Start accomplishing this by determining how much income you want—not how much you need. Here is where many agents falter. Mistakenly they focus their mind-set on the amount they need. I often hear, "I need $10,000 a month to keep up my lifestyle." Consequently with their intention firmly centered on that specific number, they wind up doing just enough to earn $10,000—and not a cent more.

Let's theorize for a moment. Assume you want to earn $250,000 a year. The next step is to ask about the average transactions you do and the typical median home price for your area. Compute the commission earned using those variables, add the marketing and other expenses, and calculate how many deals you must close in order to earn the take-home pay you want. Don't forget to factor in the taxes.

When all is computed, you may want to back out of your original goal, or perhaps totally gut it. Let's imagine you do 20 transactions annually to meet your objective. First you should investigate your closing ratios. If you make x amount of phone calls, set x amount of appointments, and bring x amount of closes to the table, you have to take into consideration what you have to do every single month to hit the $250,000 desired income.

This is an extremely important exercise, yet many people don't do it. This is why I advise agents to back out of goals in order to set a new daily objective for themselves. I find that new agents have a tendency to set a goal without knowing the outcome. They'll walk into the office in the morning and announce their plan to get right on the phone to make calls without a definite focus or goal.

Getting Down to Business

When I conclude my training session at the Learning Annex, I like to ask the agents what is the one thing they are going to do to be more successful tomorrow morning when they arrive in the office. Typically an agent responds that she will make phone calls. This is not a good answer. When I ask for details, the agent stammers and is unable to tell me whom she plans to phone! After the uncertainty, I ask when she will decide. The answer is short but not sweet—"When I get on the phone," she tells me.

Of course it's definitely a poor line of attack. You must know beforehand who you will call and plan your strategy accordingly.

What many agents are missing is that once you phone people, you have to have a follow-up—a marketing plan. After a call, perhaps you want to send out thank you notes, flyers, or something that says let's keep in touch.

The idea is to formulate a plan before you pick up the phone. Decide how frequently you intend to keep in touch. Prioritize leads. Rate them as hot, cold, lukewarm, or dead, and donate your time and effort accordingly. If a person tells you he is interested in acquiring a house as soon as his healthy, active 77-year-old grandfather dies and the inheritance comes in, and another says she needs a house within two months because she is relocating for a job promotion, then don't spend all your time with the first individual and give the remnants to the second. Recognize closing potential.

Tracking Potential Clients

The difference between the novice and mediocre agents and the top producers is that the top producers recognize their client base as the most valuable part of their business. Mediocre and novice agents on the other hand, are motivated by immediate gratification—they are constantly looking for new clients.

REALTORS® should build a business with a sound structure by creating a database. I tell them to familiarize themselves with tracking programs such as TopProducer.com, GoldMine database galaxy, or an Avidian software sales tracking program. This is a way of tracking the people you speak to who are interested in real estate and collecting some general information about them.

Social Business: The Client as a Human Being

Taking the time to make some notes on a client can be a useful tool. Record his full name, address, telephone number, and email address in your database. Note the important things regarding the client's family status—single or married with children and pets? Ask the person to tell you about his hobbies. This gives you another outlet for a subtle follow-up.

I have clients who are golf aficionados, so if I come across an attention-grabbing article about the opening of a new course or the launch of cutting-edge golf clubs, I cut it out, write a personalized note, stick it in an envelope, and mail it to them. This is a nonaggressive way of conveying to a prospective client that they are important to you and you are thinking of them. It is also a way of keeping the lines of communication open. By managing your marketing in this manner you affront real estate with a studied plan like the top producers instead of the shotgun approach common to mediocre agents.

Real Estate: A Mental Tactical Strategic Strategy

I believe the essence of real estate is strategy and tactics. Therefore, I define real estate as a *mental tactical strategic strategy*. In my opinion those four words are the key to becoming a profit center in your business and I structure my business model accordingly.

- The *mental* part encompasses everything an agent has to do in preparation for a successful outcome. In other words it is the process you as an agent have to adapt in order to get yourself intact. This includes setting your intentions and using visualizations and affirmations as a means of positive reinforcement.
- The *tactical* aspect involves the acquisition of specialized knowledge. In other words—it is all that you need to learn if you want to operate your business more efficiently, and more profitably, with a better time-management style. It is the nuts and bolts that are essential to building your business.

Now that you have the knowledge, do you know when and how to use it? With strategic planning you look at real estate as a whole not just a series of leads and closings.

- *Strategic* is about timing and involves service, marketing, and setting your intentions toward the attainment of a specific goal.

- *Strategy* is the actualization of techniques, approaches, policies, and plans, all based on the knowledge acquired, and the concept of proper timing. In order to build a strong business, it is essential to draw up a blueprint that includes these four important points.

Technology Evolution— Change Acclimatization

If your business is sound and you have an unshakeable internal system and the ability to adapt to change, it doesn't matter what type of market prevails. Any good business plan has to be flexible. We all have to adjust our behavior both professionally and socially to conform to different circumstances. Be willing to accept that change often equates to improvement. Wouldn't it be idyllic if we were always on time, every time and concluded all our tasks with perfection on the first try? Of course it would—but unless we work at it and modify our flaws, it just won't happen.

I don't proclaim to be the epitome of perfection. Sometimes I schedule three appointments for showings with three different clients in good faith, and then *I* can't keep any of them. It's not a lack of commitment or intention, but unexpected circumstances, such as a closing that has more creative financing and runs three or four hours later than expected, sometimes interrupt the flow of my day. If I couldn't adapt to change, I would be in a serious predicament.

Top producers are able to understand that change has to happen—it's part of the life cycle. To deny it would only stunt the potential for growth. Even though the old way was once the best way, it just won't work today, even if it remains the easy way. You have to be able to see the innovative direction in which technology is traveling. You have to track the youth and their business growth spurts. They are smarter and have more access to detailed databases and information in general because the technology evolution is fast, broad, and taking business to new heights.

Things are not as they used to be. The world moves forward not in reverse. Ignore the change and you'll be a mediocre agent, assuming you survive. To be a top producer it is necessary to have a real forward-thinking vision. This involves being able to identify the change that is occurring. It also includes being open to the realization that if you can get on board and keep your knowledge updated by taking as many training courses as possible, you will be able to build a solid business.

Education = Income Acceleration

I am a huge believer in training at every level, especially in continuing education and learning to sharpen awareness of what other REALTORS® are doing. Gaining knowledge from the success and errors of others gives you the insight on how you can change your plan to make it work.

Often I hear people say, especially during fluctuating markets, "You're not going to be able to do that. I've already tried it and it won't work." When you hear someone make that claim, you should consider it a professional challenge. You might just have the ability to succeed where failed. Sharing her experience with you, that agent gave you the green light to go forward because she told you what to do (or not do) and how to avoid the obstacles she had to overcome.

Many times I'll offer participants at my seminars products that I promote for continuing education. It is amazing to see how their facial expressions change when I mention these products. Sometimes when I do free speaking events, people say, "I'm not going to pay for that book or CD." It's amazing to me how many people won't invest money in a learning tool that would fast-forward them to profit.

Recently I spoke to a group of REALTORS® and told them that when I was 19, a good friend of mine signed up for a real estate training program. At the time, I was in the air force earning about $400 a month. The training program cost $2,000, and I remember gasping, "No way—that's five months of my salary!"

Another friend of mine, in the same income bracket, signed up, financed it with his credit card, and became a millionaire seven years before I did. Though we are both wealthy today, he preceded me by seven years.

When I asked him what made his earning increase so quickly he told me it was that training program. I must have seemed surprised because he assured me that everything he learned in training served to move him in the right direction.

I, on the other hand, spent seven years reading every book on real estate I could get my hands on. Even though reading was important, the books were not the fast-forward way to wealth. The super-quick way was—and still is—to learn from someone who had already done it; someone who had the answers and was in a position to share what to look out for; someone who had the success quotient to show me how to walk down that path.

When I realized the validity of my friend's in-person education, I decided to enroll in the same training program that he took seven years earlier. I followed it up by taking every educational real estate course, seminar, and training program that I could find. In fact, that year, I invested more in learning than I earned. Yet as a result of what I learned, the following year, I started to make money quickly.

Every sound business plan has to include education—be it free, for a small fee, or uncomfortably costly. I have also learned that training seminars and courses are a vehicle for meeting people—often your fellow students have phenomenal ideas and experiences to share. I would have never met some of my most valuable colleagues had I not ventured into the world of upper-end training programs.

Someone who is willing to pay $10,000 for a training program certainly has a wide personal vision, a serious business plan, and unwavering commitment. In addition, it's a great networking opportunity with a person who is of like mind and shares similar goals, as opposed to networking with someone who is struggling and walking in the dark.

I'm not done yet. When students ask me if I think I need more training, I always respond, "You bet I do. I think there is so much to learn in this world. I know we always need to further our education."

The other day I was speaking with one of my attorneys and she mentioned a particular asset protection strategy of which I had never heard. As we discussed it, she told me it was relatively new due to a recent change in the related laws. I asked her to send it to me so I could familiarize myself with it and use it when needed.

All professionals need to update their knowledge and expertise. No one would consult a physician who, upon receiving his medical degree in 1960, never again picked up a medical journal. The same holds true for a CPA, attorney, or any other professional who doesn't stay on top of his field.

As a real estate professional, you need to stay on top of your profession. Aspire to be well-informed about the latest tax laws and different business strategies that perhaps you have never tried. You should be willing to give time, money, and effort to any seminar that will give you one piece of information that you can add to your tool chest of wealth-accumulating strategies. I spend a good 10–15 percent of my annual income on training because the more I know, the more I realize how much I really don't know—and the more I am aware of what I don't know, the more I want to lower that statistic.

One of my agents asked me how I differentiate between who is a valid learning source and who is out there just to make money. I believe that with the proper mind-set you can learn from everybody. I never think people are out there to "get me." For example, I was talking to a woman in a consulting session who mentioned that in 2003 she went to the "Master of Mind-set," Mark Victor Hansen's mega book marketing event. She said the event was just awful.

Curious as always, I asked her to outline why she felt so negatively about it. Her response was interesting. She told me she was turned off by the way they were selling a lot of products related to the seminar and speakers after the event. She argued that she paid $1,500 to attend the seminar and get the information she wanted, yet she was being sold one thing after another. Apparently every speaker who addressed the audience was selling something. Frustrated, she complained that the seminar turned into a marathon sales pitch.

I suggested that she change her perspective and regard the event not as a sales marathon, but as an opportunity to learn what investment opportunities people had and were making available to her— opportunities she could invest in to accelerate her income. Shocked, she admitted that she had never thought of it like that before.

Too often we are unduly concerned about what someone is trying to sell us and we question the validity of the information being offered. We forget that most programs come with a 100-percent money-back guarantee. Therefore, if you get into a training program that doesn't resonate with you, look at the guarantee policy, take advantage of it, and leave.

I have known people who have signed up for a program with a 100-percent refund guarantee, gone through the entire program, and two years later asked for a refund claiming they still had not made money therefore the program was worthless. Many vendors are willing to refund the cost. Others may openly refuse, but you won't know whether they'll refund your money unless you ask.

100 Percent Guarantee—The Refund

Not long ago a man named Ron signed up for one of my training programs in which I offered a 100-percent guaranteed refund for unsatisfied participants. The cost was $5,000. He attended the training sessions for over a year. At the end of the course, however, he discovered that his wife would not allow him to invest. In California, a wife has to sign if her husband wants to invest. Because he could not purchase any property, he asked me for a refund. When I refused to return his money, he got angry.

When he spoke to me about it, I asked him if he liked the information he received from my program, and if he thought it was valuable and applicable. He said he did, so I asked, "Then why should I refund your money, 18 months after you took the program?"

He responded that the knowledge he acquired was useless to him because he never got to purchase any property.

The 100-percent guarantees are there for a reason. Read carefully the stipulations presented with the program. Some will refund after several hours, others will require full participation. As someone attending a seminar or training program, you have to take responsibility for the choices you make.

If you attend classes, seminars, and training programs with the right mind-set, you will come away with new knowledge. I believe everyone has something to offer. I read numerous books on real estate, although many are similar, I look for that one thing that makes the purchase, and the time spent reading, worthwhile. In addition, buying books for your business and attending training programs, seminars, and courses is a clever tax-deduction strategy!

Never Too Old to Learn New Tricks

Selling in any market involves more than attitude and mentality. There are well-defined market conditions to explore and consider. One of the best sources to consult is the National Association of REALTORS®. They have great up-to-date information and offer wonderful training. Moreover, they are open to answering your questions. Many agents who attend seminars and programs don't understand what is being discussed, so they shrug their shoulders and walk out. In the end, their lack of comprehension leads to passing on erroneous information. All they had to do to avoid this pitfall was ask a question, but many agents believe they are beyond learning.

It is never too late to learn—and yes, you can teach an old dog, new tricks. However, that old dog has to be willing to learn. Without this conviction and commitment, it just won't happen.

In one of my California seminars, a woman in her mid-60s told me she had been in the real estate business for over 30 years. After the seminar, she approached me and said she believed that something I suggested in my seminar was absolutely wrong. I had suggested REALTORS® should help their clients find money to buy property. She could not understand how that could be possible.

I explained to her that agents could show potential buyers whom a company or organization employs how to change their exemptions. Most are unaware they are entitled to up to 15 exemptions.

Defensively, she told me I was advising illegal schemes. "Exemptions have to be legal." she said.

"I'm sorry," I responded, "but you are in error. It is legal. The IRS says you can have up to fifteen."

She insisted it was absolutely not true and that I was wrong. She argued with me until I put an end to it, telling her I was there to neither debate nor argue with her. My objective was to offer her an opportunity to explore something new and different. I suggested she contact her tax attorney or CPA as soon as possible to confirm my money-saving advice. I was just asking her to explore the opportunity.

I walked across the room and asked if there was CPA in attendance. A gentleman raised his hand. I approached him and asked for verification. "The IRS allows fifteen exemptions, right?" I asked. "Right!" came his short, direct response.

Nevertheless, the woman kept stubbornly arguing her point of view, which had been confirmed as incorrect. Apparently she was a know-it-all who nonetheless had decided to sign up for my training. I didn't know why she bothered to come because she seemed so dead-set against learning anything she didn't already know.

At the end of the seminar I asked all the participants why they came and what they hoped to obtain from the session to feel if their time was well spent. The know-it-all raised her hand and asked if the class was about bubble-proof strategies at all—or just about this "mind stuff."

Trying desperately hard not to burst into laughter, I told her that if she could possibly hang in long enough she would eventually realize it was about strategies. Moreover, that to have a successful mind-set was the most important strategy of all.

This woman had come to a training session looking for strategies on how to sell better in a changing market, yet she was resisting the very person to whom she came to for this information. Resisting my advice, she had dug her heels into the mud, and at the end of the seminar I mentioned that the Learning Annex had provided a huge discount on the diverse products that I was offering. One program was being offered at an incredible reduction of thousands of dollars.

Once again, the know-it-all sighed loudly and said sarcastically, "Sure this is a discount!" I laughed—I knew what she was insinuating. The truth was that I didn't make a dime from any of it. I had volunteered to come and share my expertise with other serious REALTORS®.

After I was finished, she approached me, thanked me, and told me the seminar had been very enjoyable. She added that she realized we didn't agree because she had more experience than I did.

This narrow mind-set is what keeps people from selling in a fluctuating market. They are not open to seeing their own faulty thinking and unwilling to learn what might be true among all the notions they previously believed were false. This is a huge mistake among those REALTORS® who operate within a network of hearsay. "Well I heard the other agent say, and so and so told me." However, it never crosses their mind to pick up the phone to call an attorney or consult a professional at the National Association of REALTORS® (NAR) to get confirmation of what they've heard.

6

Calculating Power: Making Money by Understanding Money

*"Motivate them, train them, care about them,
and make winners out of them...they'll treat the customers right.
And if customers are treated right, they'll come back."*

—J. Marriott Jr.

When educating agents to become more profitable in their business, the first thing that comes to mind is the need to adapt a proper mind-set. This I define as intent, attitude, and approach—all of which are vital components of the success equation. Having tried and tested this through years of experience, I like to use the knowledge that I acquired to open the mind of every individual whose objective is to attain a higher level of success.

I intend to accomplish this goal by asking agents to forget their old way of thinking and focus on a willingness to explore something new and different. After all, the old way got them to this point in their professional lives; only gutting and rebuilding their thought process will take them beyond their current status and into a new level of earning.

Most books written for real estate professionals teach agents how to generate business in a task-oriented way. They emphasize how to organize and conduct an open house, as well as how to use listing and prospecting strategies such as door-knocking, farming, and cold-calling to increase business. I will not dispute the importance of having these tools handy, but I strongly believe that even the best tools are not effective without what I consider to be the core training.

With core training, you learn new ways of thinking and reset boundaries to broaden your possibilities and generate results whereas old thinking traps you. If you are dissatisfied with where you are today—blame it on this old thinking.

I cannot overemphasize the importance of educating yourself in order to educate your clients. I will also continue to stress that the best way to excel both in selling and buying is to have personally experienced the process. This means getting involved in the investing part. Experience the client end of deal-closing —acquire property for yourself and sell it. The most profitable agents depositing the most and the biggest commission checks are the REALTOR®-investors; well-informed professionals who have not only studied the principles of lucrative investing but have flipped their learning into deals.

My seminars teach agents a simple formula that has worked for me:

Education + Experience + Action = Results

The Tool Chest: Formulas

Agents should learn how to use technology to serve their clients better. There are many resources to help REALTORS® determine how prospective buyers can save money, thus having sufficient funds to put toward a down payment or use to obtain property with a high mortgage.

Agents should invest in a financial calculator. Tcalc.com is designed specifically for real estate computations. Learn how to use the mortgage payment calculator to compute a qualifying debt ratio which includes the PITI—principle, interest, taxes, and insurance. By entering in the sales price of the listed property and the down payment you can then select several diverse mortgage rates to compute monthly payments. I actually had a woman in one of my recent training seminars who had no idea what I was describing while I was explaining the PITI.

Surprisingly, she had been in the business for almost two decades. What she and many other agents do is give the job of computing the monthly mortgage payments to the lenders. Yet it is so easy—and much more professional—to utilize online calculators or order a handheld calculator. Don't rely on others to do your job. It will slow you down and result in the forfeiture of many potentially good deals. Calculating a client's mortgage payment puts you in a position to begin the property search while you are still waiting for the approval process to be completed. With all the diverse loan programs today, most people will complete the mortgage qualifying process on a positive note. However if time is lost because you are unable or unwilling to determine the financial aspect of their quest, you can be certain they will seek the services of a well-educated agent who will step in causing you a serious penalty: a lost deal and perhaps several referrals.

Many REALTORS® say, "I'm not going to waste my time showing properties to people who aren't qualified." My response is, "A qualified, professional commission-generating guru uses new thinking in planning a strategy: 'I can get anyone qualified, so let's find you a property.'"

Client Qualification 101

There are a few very basic but important things to know when you meet a client. To begin with, determine if you have an active buyer, a window shopper with a free cruising day, a motivated seller, or a seller trying to calculate the worth of her estate by calling in a REALTOR®.

Once you have weeded out the time-wasters and people looking for complimentary appraisals, then you can dedicate your efforts to the deal closer. At this point you should determine what category of buyer you have. I have a checklist of items I use when educating agents. This includes a course of action that will facilitate the qualifying process.

- Credit—Involve your client in the process by asking the right questions:
  - What is your credit history?
  - Do you have good credit?
  - What do you think your credit score is?
  - When was the last time you or someone else ran a credit check?
  - Can you give me at least an estimate, a ballpark figure?
  - Have you been delinquent or made any late payments within the last 30 days?
  - How is your yearly profile?
  - What is your credit identity?
  - Do you have any equity loans or line of credit?

- In the last six months have you been late or delinquent with your mortgage payments? If so, how many times has this occurred in a three-year period?
- Employment and Income History—Prequalify clients for a specific market by inquiring about their employment, earnings, and investment portfolios. If you have a client whose combined family income is just above $150,000 don't waste time and energy showing properties for which they will fail to obtain mortgage approval. In joint ownership, inquire about the other partner's income and employment profile.
- Mortgage Payments—Be an investigator. Ask about the down payment. Determine how much they can comfortably put down on a property. Explore how you can help them increase their down payment and lower their monthly mortgage responsibility. Inquire about their comfort zone with respect to monthly payments.
- Tax Deductions—There are over 350 legal tax deductions—business, personal, medical (Archer MSAs—medical savings accounts, individual health insurance premiums, long-term care premiums, nursing home care for ailing parents), dental, self-employed, casualty, theft, involuntary conversion, interest (investment, business, personal, student loans, passive activity, mortgage), loan origination fee or points, charitable (cash and noncash), taxes (local, state, and foreign income, sales, real estate, and property) and even gambling losses, available which can put extra money on the table for a down payment. As a professional, you should fully investigate a client's options or have a tax specialist ready to refer.
- Prequalification—Ask your clients if they have been prequalified. If not, prepare a debt to income formula. This will help determine the percentage of income accessible for the

mortgage. Learn how to apply the 28/36 qualifying ratio: 28 percent household expenditures and 36 percent household expenditures plus recurring debt (long-term financial commitments, i.e., credit card debt, loans, child support obligations, and alimony payments).

- Down Payment—Although many agents feel squeamish about making personal financial inquiries regarding the monetary figure for a down payment and often opt to pass it along to the lender/loan officer, it is of vital importance to get the info. You cannot search for properties if you don't know how much your clients can afford to spend on the acquisition of a house. Ask the question and get the answer so you can structure the transaction and close the deal. You will need to calculate the amount of assets required (typically three to six months of reserves are required).

Flip Showings into Closings

Always be mindful of the business truth—money is what makes the deal work. This rule will guide you from showing to closing. It is essential that your clients have the finances required—but if they are lacking, it is your job as a professional to help them find it!

Educate yourself about the loan process. Loans are the key to your success and the deal maker or breaker. Be well-informed about different loan types and learn how they work. This knowledge will enable you to deliver different options to your potential buyers.

Following are some typical loans and others that are more unusual but work just as well in certain situations.

- Pay Option Adjustable-Rate Mortgage—This type of loan is an adjustable-rate mortgage structured to offer payment elasticity to control monthly cash flow. The low initial start-up rate makes it easier for clients to qualify. The minimum payment and interest-only payment alternatives allow for more affordable payments.

- 2/28 Adjustable-Rate Mortgage—This is a 30-year mortgage with a two-year fixed rate that is variable for the remaining 28 years. It is decidedly more affordable than a 30-year fixed loan.

- Interest-Only Loan (IO)—This is a 10-year term limit interest-only loan for a 30-year mortgage with lenient qualifying requirements due to lower than fixed-rate mortgage payments. The IO offers more flexibility with respect to managing personal monthly finances.

- Adjustable Rate Mortgage (ARM)—The ARM divides the risk possibility of higher rates between the buyer and the lender. Consequently it offers lower start-up rates. This loan can be a good option in the instances of short-term ownership, elevated interest rates, and elevated income prospects.

- Lender Buydown—This type of loan has an initial discount, which slowly increases over a three-year period to a previously agreed-upon fixed rate.

- Reduction Option Loan (ROL)—This is a convertible fixed-rate mortgage. With this type of loan, buyers can get an adjusted lower interest rate with a small payment and a minimal loan amount-based fee, in some cases just about a quarter of a percentage point.

- Reverse Annuity Mortgage (RAM)—This type of loan is tailored to older homebuyers at least 62 years old. The lender appraises the property and the loan is calculated according to a percentage of its market value. This profits the homeowner by furnishing a monthly tax-free income.

- Seller-Assisted Creative Financing—This loan is structured to allow the seller to participate in the financing by underwriting all or part of the loan. This is a lower-rated loan with lower monthly payments.
- Fixed-Rate Mortgage (FRM)—With this loan, both the interest rate and monthly mortgage payments remain fixed for the duration of the loan. Fixed-rate mortgages can be for 10, 15, 20, 25, 30, or more years; usually the shorter the term of a loan, the lower the interest rate.
- Balloon Loan—This type of loan is a short-term fixed rate mortgage with fixed monthly payments generally based upon a 30-year fully amortizing plan in addition to an end-of-term lump-sum payment.

Because the loan process plays a major role in making deals successful, I recommend getting a loan option education and making connections with well-informed lenders. Each loan broker probably specializes in five different types of loans. I have listed several above, however I advise agents to research and become knowledgeable about the many loan options available. There are the standard mortgage plans, the more creative, and the ultimate resourceful.

Myth Versus Truth

Myth: Paying off your mortgage and owning your property free and clear is the most advantageous way to go. You have peace of mind knowing you are debt free. How advantageous is this method with respect to your finances, however? Without a mortgage you don't have a tax deduction for mortgage interest.

Truth: Paying off your home/investment reaps very little benefit. This promortgage theory promotes the idea that a good financial strategy involves getting a mortgage with the lowest monthly payments possible, refinancing as rates dip, and prolonging paying off the loan. This plan will create tax deductions, increase cash flow, and increase earning potential from eventual property appreciation.

REALTORS® need to learn and keep learning—you can never get enough education. Learn the tax laws, be able to discuss and explain to your clients how owning property and paying a mortgage will give them tax deductions just as charitable contributions do. Inform them that loan proceeds are nontaxable.

A buyer can refinance an existing property, keep the proceeds, and still qualify for a tax deduction. On the other hand it is important to consider that property with equity has no ROI (return on investment) whereas money invested does.

For example, you invest $200,000 in a rental apartment located in the business and entertainment center of a city. The unit has a market value of $1.2 million and a $1-million mortgage. After expenses (mortgage, taxes, insurance, HOA fees, and assessment payments) you net $4,150 a month. Your ROI is 25 percent. Then time passes and markets soften and harden. Several years later, the same property is worth $1.5 million based on the building/neighborhood comps reporting current sales. Although you raised the rent along the way, you now come away with $4,750 a month. In the meantime, you have paid off $100,000 of the mortgage. Now you discover that just a few years later your ROI has depreciated to 10.36 percent! The equity in the property has increased but not in line with your ROI.

The lesson here is to determine and understand the true worth of rental property. This will help in calculating the earning potential and setting a value on the investment. If a red light flashes, then it's time to rethink this investment and seek more property investment training.

Always remember that money tied up in property is at risk. When the market fluctuates, equity goes up and down. If instead of tying it up, you put it in an investment with a conservative 8-percent return then your profit involves the power of compounding and security plus the availability of tax deductions. There is always the factor of property appreciation and the cash flow to ride out the cycles. In addition, you are in prime position to sell at top dollar. Prospective buyers preview properties with an eye for what is owed to see if financing can be carried.

Tax Deductions 101

Another important factor to consider is finding a client more money with which to enter into a transaction. One of the best ways to accomplish this is to research and study the plethora of legal tax deductions available. Learn how to calculate tax savings. Being able to demonstrate to your clients how with the funds saved through tax deductions, they can afford to own their desired property is a powerful skill. It helps move the deal to a closing and leaves potential for referrals.

Consider after-tax calculations. Learn how to apply the formula for estimated after-tax payment. Instruct clients about depreciation and explain how taxes are paid. Clients must also understand the different filing categories:

- Single
- Married filing separately
- Married filing joint
- Head of household filing
- Trusts and estates

It is also important to understand the tax bracket formulas. Most people assume that if they are in a 15-percent tax bracket they are obliged to pay 15 percent of their income in taxes. This isn't true, of course. For example: If a client earns $30,650 he qualifies for the 15-percent tax bracket. If the following year he earns $30, 651 dollars and enters the 25-percent bracket, he is not subject to the higher rate on his total earning. Instead, he is taxed 15 percent of every dollar for the $30,650 and 25 percent for every dollar over in excess of that amount ($1). This formula is applied as salary increases from the 15-percent bracket all the way up to 35 percent.

To facilitate an understanding of these calculations and help clients with the facts and figures, agents are advised to prepare a chart listing salaries, percentages, and tax figures for the different tax filing categories. Of course the formula applicable to an unmarried person will be different from that of a joint filing married couple or a head of household.

Be knowledgeable. Be able to show clients how they can get the much-needed tax deductions to increase their down payment and qualify for a mortgage on their desired property.

I believe in the money-accruing power of tax deductions and impress upon my clients that stashing money in the pocket of the IRS until tax return time is not a wise business decision. If you are paying taxes throughout the year, you are forfeiting the possibility to invest those dollars to earn a return. In this scenario the dividend collector is the IRS.

Point out the savings to be collected from taxes, interest, insurance, and depreciation. In order to accomplish this, an agent should be able to calculate the PITI after tax savings and depreciation have been factored in.

Do your homework. Be current and up-to-date on the latest tax exemptions laws. For instance, in 2006 there were some added deductions:

- New Telephone Tax Refund—If a federal excise tax was paid for long-distance service from February 28, 2003–August 1, 2006, a refund is merited. The U.S. Treasury estimated this refund figure to be in the $10 billion category.
- New Home Energy Credit—The Energy Policy Act rewards consumers who have turned their homes into energy efficient property with a $500 tax credit. Qualifying criteria consists of insulation, new exterior windows, hot water boiler, oil furnace, solar panels ($2,500 credit) and fuel-cell power plant.
- The Educator Expense Deduction—Teachers are given a $250 write-off for supplies.
- College Tuition Deduction—Up to $4,000 is given.

There are many IRS-sanctioned deductions and no limits regarding how many you may take as long as you qualify—consult a tax specialist.

Assessed Value Versus Price Paid

The primary factor to consider is the assessed value of the property. Often the assessed value can turn out to be less than the price you have agreed to pay for the property. If the former owner claims that the property taxes are $3,000 based on a different appraisal, it is essential to know how to calculate future tax payments using the sales contract purchase figure. When a property changes ownership, generally the assessed value increases.

All REALTORS® should get a calculator and familiarize themselves with computing the following:

- PITI
- After-tax payment
- Annual depreciation
- Appreciation

An agent who is educated and knowledgeable about these calculations will discover this skill to be valuable and profitable in concluding successful transactions. In real estate, big bucks are made by understanding how to structure a deal, obtain financing, and help clients find the money to acquire their dream homes. The paperwork is merely the bureaucratic follow-up to a successful transaction. It's how agents spend their time between post-sale and predepositing of their commission checks that matters, not before the sale.

You can gain more expertise and be able to flip all your leads into closings by signing up for and attending more classes structured on "How to be an investor." Apart from the wealth of information gained, it is a great place to meet clients and to discover all the facts and information they have at their finger tips that maybe you don't have!

Calculating Taxes

It is imperative that agents are able to explain capital gains to clients. In real estate, capital gain is defined as the tax levied on the profit arising from the appreciation of capital assets (property) above the original purchase price.

Another essential formula to have at your fingertips is the CGT, capital gains tax computation. As a professional REALTOR®, you should be able to determine the capital gains on a property. This is done by adding the price paid for the property to the amount spent on capital improvements and then subtracting that figure from the depreciation to get the net adjusted basis. From the current sales price, subtract the net adjusted basis, and then subtract the closing expenses. This yields the capital gain figure.

To determine the amount of taxes due, calculate the 25-percent depreciation recapture, the 15-percent federal capital gains, and the state capital gains, which differ from state to state. Take the current sales price and subtract the mortgage loan balances, the closing expenses, and the amount of taxes due. This equals the after-tax cash proceeds.

REALTORS® should also be able to explain:

- **1031 Exchange**—Section 1031 of the Internal Revenue Code permits a deferment of the capital gains tax. This type of tax-deferred exchange is a mechanism that allows a property owner to sell the property and be able to reinvest the funds in a "like-kind property" taking a capital gains tax deferment.
- **Passive Income**—This type of income refers to the earning arising from a property that is leased, a limited partnership deal, or any other income resulting from an inactive status.
- **Portfolio Income**—This refers to interest, dividends, and royalties from other investments.
- **Passive Loss**—This is the financial loss resulting from passive activity (i.e., a rental property, limited partnership, investments, and other income earned from a nonactive status).

It is also wise to investigate the special tax deduction under passive loss for real estate professionals as stipulated in the Revenue Reconciliation Act of 1993. One year later, however it was established that rental real estate would not qualify as passive if a real estate professional did not comply with certain standards.

- If more than 50 percent of professional services are conducted in the real estate business
- If more than 750 hours are dedicated to the real estate business
- If the agent does not hold employee status (An exception is given to an agent who has a minimum 5-percent ownership of the business.)

I like to use and recommend J.K. Lasser's *Your Income Tax 2007*. It is an excellent, best-selling manual compiled by a team of tax experts that outlines in an easy-to-read format a synopsis of the latest tax law changes. Handy and informative it also provides the necessary forms and includes a fast flip-through index leading to specific tax issues. There is also an edition specializing in real estate deductions. In addition there are other valuable tax-filing tools at jklasser.com.

Other tax incentive possibilities worth investigating include:

- **401k**—This is an employer-sponsored retirement plan that permits an employee to save for retirement while deferring income taxes on the saved money and earnings until withdrawal.
- **Private Pension Plans**—These plans involve putting money in an employer-sponsored fund to be withdrawn at retirement.
- **Defined Benefits**—This is an employer-backed retirement plan in which employee benefits are calculated using variables such as salary history and length of employment. The employer managing the portfolio assumes the investment risk.
- **Defined Contribution**—This is a retirement plan that allows the individual to turn over to an employer to invest, a specific amount or percentage of income every year. There are definite restrictions regarding withdrawals and penalties.
- **IRA Traditional and Roth**—These are participant-structured plans.

- **Tax Sheltered Annuity (TSA)**—This plan includes fixed (guaranteed) and variable annuities and mutual funds, which carry no guarantee.

Having all the facts about investments and tax deductions puts you in a better position to enable your clients to find more money to purchase their dream house. Needless to say, this equates not only to more commission checks to deposit—but also bigger ones!

7

Protecting Commissions Through Cutting-Edge Service

"The goal as a company is to have customer service that is not just the best, but legendary."

—Sam Walton

President Kennedy famously said, "Ask not what your country can do for you, but what you can do for your country." You should apply that idea to your business model under the heading of customer service because in the real estate profession, the client provides your paycheck. A satisfied client is synonymous with a closing deal just as a sale equates to a commission check.

It is essential for agents to learn how to highlight and assess a property's value, explain and convey it to clients, convincingly ask for the commissions they deserve, and provide nothing short of cutting-edge service.

Service is so important because in a sense, service is like lubricating oil—it loosens the rust and grime that prevent a transaction from running smoothly and efficiently. It removes the rough edges and works through the initial creases.

Structuring the Client-Agent Relationship

Service means not only listening to your clients, but also encouraging them to express their wants, needs, disappointments, and criticisms. If a client takes the time to complain and expends his energy to outline what he feels is missing from your business presentation, it means you are valued as an agent. You can accomplish this objective simply by designing your business plan around the client as your priority. This is accomplished by:

- Exploring client expectations—Establish what your client expects from you as a professional and adjust your plan to guarantee you will neither disappoint nor fall short. Clients are people, and people are as different as night and day. Never assume all buyers and sellers are created equal. This is a real estate fallacy. Some clients require an agent's undivided attention and seek constant feedback, answers to their questions, and an escort to accompany them through the sales process. Others prefer to preview in silence without any agent participation.
- Soliciting client feedback—Once you have determined needs, wants, and expectations, encourage client comments. Ask them if they are satisfied with the buying/selling process and how you

could make the transaction smoother. There is always room for improvement!

- Building trust—Act with sincerity, openness, and integrity, and always in the best interest of the client. Be precise and reliable in your day to day dealings. Consistency helps develop trust. Convey to your clients that all your decisions are based exclusively on the benefits they will receive.

- Listening to your clients—Disgruntled or unhappy clients will just walk away in silence and phone another agent. Therefore, learn how to accept criticism as good advice and act upon it to change your professional behavior.

For example if a client tells you she feels it is a waste of time to visit 10 properties in one day because she cannot absorb too many floor plans, schedule three per day. Some people prefer to take notes when visiting properties and like to remain on-site a bit longer. If you rush them through the process confusion and frustration will override a closing. In a way you are working for them and if you do it their way then your time and efforts will be compensated with a commission check and perhaps a referral.

If your client asks a question regarding a matter that you believe isn't part of your job, then renovate your job description and make it your job to know the answer. A little effort and the willingness to change old habits will present a new opportunity for delivering optimum service. This in turn demonstrates your value as an agent.

Client-Agent Relationship Maintenance

Be there for your buyer or seller! If your client has qualms about the escrow paperwork, or if he is confused and has questions or expresses frustration because he is unable to understand the different aspects of the transaction, be willing to extend your service agreement. Add into the agreement that you will personally contact the escrow company and pose the questions on behalf of your client or set up a three-party conference to allow your client to get informed firsthand while you are available to ask additional questions.

When a client asks a question you are unable to answer, don't just let it drop with silence or a "Gee that's a good one—you got me there!" Tell the client you will get back to him as soon as possible with an answer. This is why I repeat over and over again the value of education. Getting the answers to unknown questions will allow you to avoid an embarrassing situation the next time around. Be willing to learn by taking inventory of your real estate knowledge. Even seasoned REALTORS® need to sign up for and attend continuing education courses and seminars. Learning never stops, and as a professional you will never know it all.

Agents Are Not on Sale

Money spent is rarely if ever regretted or discussed if the product or service is top of the line. Clients will be less likely to refuse your commission requests when they recognize your worth through the service you deliver both during and after the transaction. There is a very strong correlation between price and value. Everyone is willing to spend for quality service and merchandise. Therefore, I encourage agents to balance the commission with service. No one will question your commission rates if you demonstrate the reasoning of your actions. Show clients why you deserve a high commission.

Agents should never underestimate their professional worth. Always be willing to give the best service possible. Treat commissions as a negotiable reward for top-notch commitment to a client. Some agents feel they will loose a deal if they don't discount their commission. Not so—in fact commission haggling is a rather unproductive tactic. In addition to reducing earnings, this bargaining tool depreciates the agent's value.

However, if you default on the quality and quantity of your service, clients will be unwilling to agree to a commission percentage without taking it to the bargaining table.

Cutting-Edge Service: Dos and Don'ts

During my seminars, I have had the opportunity to meet many agents who approached me afterwards and inquired if I had a magic formula for my cutting-edge service. I explained that I had a business plan that included certain aspects of the real estate process that I would implement for the advantage of my clients and myself as an agent. I responded there were several dos and don'ts from which an agent should never stray.

Dos:

- Provide clear typewritten documents for their signature.
- Be accessible to pick up the appraisal check if the client is unavailable to do so. This seemingly insignificant gesture will make the process easier for her and show your professional savvy.
- Be an excellent listener. It's about the clients—not you. Ask the right questions and stop talking when they outline their needs and wants. If you don't know what they are looking for, then there is no way you can be instrumental in helping them find it.
- Be available. Make it easy for clients to contact you. If feasible, get a separate 1-800 toll-free line for complaints and comments.

There are many Internet servers offering free email addresses. Get one with a large inbox for messages and attachments. Get another for complaints; if you categorize it will be easier, quicker, and more reliable for you to respond to them. Regardless of the contact method be certain to display the information on all your marketing collaterals such as business cards, postcards, brochures, stationary, and websites.

- Get into the habit of sending a token "welcome to your new home" gift together with your business card. Gifts should be comparable with the commission earned and the lifestyle of the clients, for instance; a plant, a bottle of wine or champagne, or some other more innovative gift such as a chocolate house or champagne bottle decorated with the new owner's name. As an agent, you will be remembered and referred.

- Implement a follow-up strategy. Take the time to ask for feedback. About a week or 10 days after a closing make it a habit to phone, send an email, or write a postcard. Thank them for engaging you as their agent and inquire if they were pleased with your way of doing business. If not, ask for their suggestions and reassure them the same issues will not recur in the future. You cannot correct an unknown error.

- Encourage comments. Hand clients a typed performance evaluation questionnaire. When they return it, take the time to thank them for their time and any compliments they offered and discuss their less-than-praising feedback. Often written surveys can be vague, and sometime people don't have the time, ability, or desire to write lengthy epistles. This may force you to forfeit some very helpful and important constructive criticism.

A top-notch agent strives to demonstrate that he runs a first-class real estate business that prioritizes the client not the broker. It's about the clients and their families. They are your commission check—they are your business.

Don'ts:

- Don't ask clients to write their own cancellation letters. Instead present it ready for signature.
- Never lose your composure with clients. You are a professional and it is a good idea to demonstrate knowledge, experience, and expertise, instead of bouts of frustration, confusion, incompetence, and exaggerated nonchalance.
- Never verbally agonize about how busy, overwhelmed, sought after, or stressed-out you are from an overload of work. This ploy does not give the impression of a REALTOR® in high demand with an overloaded appointment calendar. Instead this type of '*pseudo* VIP agent' presentation sends a message that you are far too busy to dedicate quality time to them.

Your clients should be convinced beyond a reasonable doubt that they are your primary concern. This should be conveyed not by words but through actions. Greet them and treat them with style and class. It is the service quotient of your business that distinguishes you from other agents and likewise that which elevates you to a top-notch professional as well as transforms you into a phenomenal profit center!

Commission Validation

In order to justify your commission, structure and operate your real estate activity with the same mind-set and planning as you would any other business venture. Don't utilize a *carpe diem* philosophy that perceives only the moment. Instead widen your vision—aim and plan for longevity.

Professional careers consume a great segment of life—they are often a major part of who we are as individuals. Therefore, your business should be taken seriously and with the objective to grow, develop, and thrive in time.

It's not just about closing a transaction. It's about building a reputation as a serious professional. It's about referrals, repeat business, and the ability to ask for and get higher commissions.

The best way to secure your career as a successful REALTOR® is to design and implement a business model. This task includes setting intentions, targeting a goal, and plotting strategies that will enable you to not only reach your objective but also to go beyond into new territory.

There are several steps to consider when designing a business model. Most important is to get to know your clients. Conduct a brief introductory interview. Find out how they would prefer to do business with you.

For example, ask them straight out, "How do you like to conduct your business?" Let them know your focus is on helping them accomplish their goal in a manner that best suits their busy lifestyle.

Advise agents not to be afraid to *ask* questions and to be willing to *listen* to the responses. Speak with your clients and ask them how they wish to be served. Once you have gathered the information, reassure your buyers/sellers that your business model includes the intention to make the process as pleasurable, efficient and accommodating as possible.

If they have any suggestions or preferences regarding how they wish to be contacted—via either phone calls and/or emails—be willing to adjust your business model to fit their needs and requirements. You neither want to badger nor exasperate prospects with torrents of unread or unwanted emails and phone calls.

Always make yourself client-accessible. After all, potential home-buyers are excited and interested *now,* not next week or in a year. Understand the value of being at a client's disposal. It's essential to remember:

- Accessibility and availability demonstrate a quality of service that goes beyond the norm.
- Accessibility means the client gets *you* when she phones—not an impersonal computerized message or your voice recording.

Be prepared to multitask and handle different situations. If you are out in the field showing properties at a specific point in the day, be conscientious about giving your buyers/sellers an appropriate time frame within which they can ring you. However, unpredictable circumstances do arise, and if you are with another client and a call goes to voicemail be certain to return it as soon as possible. The same holds true for emailing and paging. This diligent work ethic tells clients you are a first-rate professional intent on pleasing them.

Showing Instructions

Another factor to take into consideration is how you show properties. Discuss and familiarize yourself with how your clients prefer to preview properties. Some people tend to favor the independent approach. They want to be on their own as soon as you open the entry door. Perhaps they like to roam around unaccompanied, to get a feel for the place. In silence they hope to explore the sounds and smells of the new environment. Here is where REALTORS® make serious mistakes and often loose sales! They foolishly believe they have to "sell" the property while annoyingly tailgating the potential buyers from room to room making comments or expressing personal opinions and thoughts that are both unsolicited and unwanted.

Always remember: it's about the client—the client is the one who is going to live in the house so let the client form his own opinions and make the decisions. Instead of aggressively hounding buyers, flip to a more nurturing approach. Persuade clients to take their time and visit and revisit every room and aspect of the property. Encourage them to envision themselves living in the house and enjoying the yard and family room while you step aside and allow them the unhurried freedom to get acclimated with the surroundings. Let them bond with the property—and let them actually fall in love with it! Emotions play a major role in the decision-making process.

What you don't want to do is spoil the house-client relationship development that could make or break the sale with constant unwelcome chatter that confuses, disturbs, and may turn off a buyer.

The best way to approach a showing is to tell a client as you are nearing the house, "There are some very distinctive features about this property which I will be willing to share with you at your request." Let the client know you are going to step aside but that you are available to answer any questions while on site or at a later moment.

This courtesy gives clients the option to choose your intervention and the security of knowing they have selected the right agent who is truly interested in extending a *ne plus ultra* service over and beyond the mediocre agent. By so doing you will solidify your relationship and navigate the transaction toward the closing table.

In my almost two decades as a REALTOR®, investor, and educator I have more often than not seen agents make the decision regarding how they will undertake the house-hunting process without taking the time to inquire if in effect their way is the most agreeable to the client. Everyone is different. You don't want to implement a formula that will frustrate or annoy your client. This is one sure way to lose a transaction and give another agent your commission check when the distraught buyer/seller engages the services of another REALTOR®. Remember: the objective is to satisfy your clients, validate your commissions, and gain referral business.

Keep a database with all the information you collected from your clients regarding their business preferences, what they expect from you, and their objectives and needs. This will save time and error when dealing with the same clients at a later date. In your list also include their preferences; likes and dislikes; fears and concerns; comments and criticisms; family members; needs and requests; and hobbies and passions. Include these personal facts plus your own impressions and comments in a file. Taking the time to complete a profile will enable you to keep in contact.

For example, if you have a client who expressed a desire for a house with a spacious state of the art kitchen because preparing gourmet meals is an essential part of her life, and you happen to discover a great recipe authored by a renowned Food Channel chef, take the time to forward it via email or a handwritten note saying, "I ran across this recipe and knowing your flair for innovative gourmet creations, I thought you might like to give it a try."

This gracious personal gesture keeps the lines of communication open, but more importantly it keeps your name buzzing through heads and gives your business card a well-merited reprieve from its recycle bin destiny!

Quality service leads to commissions in quantity. Many people reward excellent agents with repeat business. Instead of stashing your card under mounds of junk mail destined for the trash, they will file it in the top draw of their desk for easy reference should the occasion present itself.

Dare to Step Beyond

We have discussed specific strategies that will validate your commission check. Yet it is also wise to learn how commissions are forfeited in order to avoid losing business and destroying your reputation.

Never ask prospects if they are currently working with another agent. Instead, demonstrate your particular business style or brand. Be willing and available to answer their questions and graciously share with them all of the information they request. Set yourself above the average. Assume every prospect is a potential client and looking for a top-notch agent. Dare to be different and always available to walk one step beyond mediocre REALTORS®.

Offer all prospects quality service right from the initial "hello," and treat them as if they had already made the decision to engage you as their agent. In refusing to work for prospects until they sign a professional agreement, many agents make a serious mistake. The moment they realize the prospect is working with another agent, they slam down the receiver, instead of listening and just being accommodating by giving multiple listing and price information.

In my experience as an investor, I find that when I tell agents that I am in touch with another agent, they tell me to contact the other for the information I am seeking! I shake my head and think to myself; "How utterly rude and unprofessional!"

This demonstrates not only discourteous behavior but is also a statement of poor business strategy. In slamming the phone down, they forfeited the potential to close on their own listings. If by chance I needed to make a referral somewhere down the line, that agent would be the last REALTOR® I would take into consideration. Consequently the bout of selfishness may have caused them to lose even more commission checks.

Another strategy to avoid involves speaking on a cell phone in the company of clients. Many agents fail to realize that a mobile conversation can be overhead when in close proximity. Perhaps they speak in one way to the client then contradict themselves when talking to a loan officer or another agent. This tactic provides an irredeemable appraisal of an agent's integrity and is an irreparable reputation destroyer.

8

Tax Savvy 101: Tax Dollars or Investment Income

"The avoidance of taxes is the only intellectual pursuit that carries any reward."

—John Maynard Keynes

In order to make money, you have to invest money—but in order to invest money you have to have money! Sound like a paradox that will keep you from investing? Not if you learn how to inflate your bank account by turning your commission check dollars into investment income and structuring your professional life to command more dollars in your pocket.

Earning Money on the Money You Earn

The best way to have more money in hand is to investigate the full gamut of tax-saving strategies that are open to real estate agents. There

are numerous avenues for accumulating wealth. Among these financially lucrative approaches are limited liability companies, charitable
contributions, and the formation of private foundations.

- **Limited Liability Company**—An LLC is a business model that
  amalgamates the cross taxation of a partnership or sole proprietorship with the limited liability of a corporation. In an LLC
  the owners divulge business profits or losses on their personal
  income tax returns. However, the LLC is not treated as a separate taxable unit. Like owners of a corporation, LLC owners are
  sheltered from personal liability arising from business debts and
  claims—thus the name, "limited liability." With an LLC only
  business assets are jeopardized if debts or lawsuits ensue. Personal property is left untouched.

- **Charitable Contributions**—Deductions can be granted if gifts
  are entered on the 1040 Schedule A form. To be valid, contributions must be made to reputable organizations and institutions.
  This includes federal, state, and local government agencies
  and organizations that are structured to operate for charitable,
  religious, artistic, educational, and scientific purposes as well as
  those advocating the prevention of abuse and/or cruelty toward
  children and animals.

- **Charitable Remainder Trusts**—These are another method
  of allotting funds or other property to a charity or organization while receiving income during your lifetime and reap-
  ing significant tax benefits connected with charitable trusts.
  The charitable remainder trust is an irreversible transfer of assets to a trustee. It is exercised through a trust agreement and
  works by investing the assets on behalf of the income recipient
  who receives the payments. The income beneficiary can be
  either self-appointed or entrusted to others. When the trust is

terminated, due to death or the expiration of a predetermined period of time as stipulated in the agreement, the residual trust assets are applied to a predetermined charity. There are two categories of charitable remainder trusts: annuity and unitrust. They differ predominately in the calculating of payments to the recipient.

- **Private Nonprofit Foundations**— The U.S. Internal Revenue has a provision, 501(c), which classifies the various types of nonprofit organizations that qualify as organizations with some federal income exemptions. If you check Sections 503 through 505 you will gain information regarding the requirements necessary to apply for such exemptions. For example: 501(c)(3) exemptions are applicable to corporations, and any community fund or foundation structured and operated solely for charitable, religious, scientific, and educational purposes as well as the defense, betterment, and protection of citizens and animals. It also applies to nonprofits established to encourage national or international amateur sports competition.

- **Private Annuity Trusts**—These trusts grant property owners a postponement regarding their fiscal responsibility in the paying of capital gains taxes on the sale of their property. With this type of trust, the homeowner transfers ownership of the property over to a trust. In return, the trust presents the owner with a payment contract, acknowledged as a private annuity. It is agreed by the conditions of the trust that regular payments will be made to the owner over his life time. Afterwards, the private annuity trust is at liberty to liquidate the property for a cash settlement.

- **1031 Exchange**—They are far from complicated to understand and apply but 1031s require a basic knowledge of the mechanism and a willingness to accept the principle of reinvesting to defer capital gains taxes. A 1031 tax deferred exchange is opportune for an investor who is selling one property and intentioned on reinvesting the earnings from that sale into one or more new investment properties. There is another component to the equation—a reputable intermediary, whose role involves holding the proceeds of the sale and completing the necessary paperwork. Consequently the investor defers paying capital gains taxes by reinvesting the revenue from the sale of one property into another investment property.

Accumulating More Money

During the process of accumulating wealth, saving money is as equally vital as earning money. Based on this philosophy, I provide agents and all those who attend my training seminars specific and detailed guidelines regarding the quickest and most efficient ways to create and sustain wealth. I take it a step further and outline and explain the mechanism of taxes—what must be paid to remain a free citizen and what can be legally deducted keeping Uncle Sam happy. I also emphasize the importance of education to develop an in-depth understanding and working knowledge of the principles of taxation and how certain errant strategies can actually deplete your income needlessly.

If you are not sufficiently tax savvy to counter each income level you may reach with the appropriate category of expense, then you will repeatedly find yourself overpaying the IRS. Of course, these tax-saving strategies aren't just for you. Helping clients save money equates to earning a bigger commission check by giving them the extra cash they need for the down payment on their dream house. In educating your clients regarding their finances, you also learn how to accumulate more money. This is why it is essential to be knowledgeably and aware of all the tax saving opportunities available to property owners.

A successful strategy is to suggest a change in the W-2 exemptions. It is not good investing for them to entrust their hard-earned dollars to the IRS until they are ready to file for a refund. Educate clients on ways to put their money into the property, qualify for a tax deduction, and be in a stronger position to afford and carry the property because they opted to withhold it from the IRS!

Investigating tax laws will lead you to the realization that one of the major tax deductions open to property owners is the primary residence deduction. As a REALTOR® it is to your benefit to emphasize that homeownership permits some substantial tax advantages that would be nonexistent in rental-lease agreement because a property owner can deduct points utilized to get a mortgage when purchasing a home, and deduct the mortgage interest payments during the year, as well as the property taxes.

Home Acquisition Debt Versus Home Equity Debt

Understanding the IRS property deduction clauses enables you to be more successful in convincing your clients to purchase instead of lease their primary residence. Become informed about the home acquisition debt. Be aware and prepared to tell your clients that any first or second mortgage obtained to purchase, build, or rehab a property is grouped under a home acquisition debt. There is another loophole the IRS catalogs as "home equity debt." Essentially, this equates to any loan figure that exceeds the actual dollar amount spent to buy, build, or renovate the property.

Once again if a buyer gets cash out while refinancing the home, whatever figure above the primary mortgage is categorized as home equity debt with the exception of the funds applied toward rehabbing the property. This formula is valid in the case of second mortgages with the same conditions: renovations, betterments, and improvements are excluded. However, in order to be eligible to deduct the interest, the equity debt must be equal to or less than $100,000. In addition, the total mortgage debt on the house cannot exceed the actual property value.

Installment Sale Strategy

The advantage of selecting an installment sale is that it is beneficial to both sellers and buyers. This type of transaction involves the selling of a property at a gain where at minimum one payment is due following the tax year in which the sale takes place. The buyer or seller is under obligation to report the sale utilizing the installment method. The only exception is if the party opts out during the sale year.

When the buyer or seller chooses to opt out they are required to report all of the profit as income in the year of the sale. It is important to understand that losses are not factored in installment sale rules. In other words, the installment method cannot be a working strategy to report profit from the liquidation of inventory or stocks and securities traded on a recognized securities market.

The installment sale is used to create a secure and steady stream of income. If the seller is willing to "carry paper" then he or she will be able to build a profitable rate of return and cross collateralize his or her note to another property or diminish the risk by being in a secondary position.

The installment method works as follows: If you choose to follow the route of the installment method, every year you are eligible to report just a percentage of the profit earned or is estimated to have been earned plus the interest. The profit will be taxed at the current maximum federal tax rate of 15 percent for capital gains, plus state tax.

The installment sale parcels out the capital gains tax over the years you receive principal payments from the buyer. The buyer's promissory note is protected by a recorded mortgage or deed of trust on the property sold.

If the buyer defaults you can foreclose to either regain your property and list it to sell for a second profit, or exercise the option to have a sizeable bidder at the foreclosure sale satisfy the loan in full. As the seller of a property, you benefit from the installment sale by earning a higher interest rate with security, currently at least 6 percent. However, this interest is taxed as standard income.

As a buyer's agent the installment sale translates to less-complicated financing, because your client is exempt from the mortgage qualifying process. Consequently you can list the property for big bucks and not have your buyer refused because the financing has been already acquired.

To report an installment sale, the IRS has a special form 6252 to facilitate the process. In addition you are required to file the standard IRS form utilized to report your income tax, and attach form 4797 and Schedule D.

Going for Maximum Draw: HELOC Versus Home Equity Loan

A HELOC, or home equity line of credit, is a loan set up as a line of credit for maximum draw, as opposed to a prestabilized dollar amount. Using this strategy, the lender agrees to lend a maximum amount of money for an agreed term. As collateral the borrower puts up the equity in his property to guarantee the loan.

The HELOC differs from the standard home equity loan in that the borrower does not receive the full amount up front. Instead the line of credit is used to borrow the funds, which do not exceed the amount. When a property closes a specific credit line is determined that establishes the maximum amount available. In a way, the mechanism is similar to putting a home purchase on a credit card. A home equity loan serves to fill your pocket with a specified dollar amount all in one lump sum. This type of refinancing is basically a second mortgage, and as such is solidified with a fixed interest rate and monthly payments. In addition, payment of the loan can be within a 30-year period. However, some mortgage companies do have rate reduction programs to decrease monthly obligations if certain terms and conditions are met. Once again as an educated agent aware of the various financing options available you are in a better position not only to help your clients complete the best transaction possible but also to use the information to your own financial benefit.

If a borrower is intentioned to obtain diverse amounts over an unspecified period of time and be able to write checks, the HELOC is the best way to go. This works by immediately securing the loan after getting approved. Unlike the home equity loan, however, should you require additional money, you can borrow up to your available credit line while you advance with your loan payment obligations. In general, the minimum monthly payment equates to the interest charge on the loan.

Most companies offer fixed-interest HELOCs, which allow monthly responsibility to remain stable even when interest rates fluctuate. Therefore if you need extra cash you can continue to borrow at the interest rate fixed when you secured the line of credit. Perhaps this is why HELOC loans are frequently secured. Not only is the easy cash draw an attractive feature but if certain conditions are satisfied the interest is deductible under federal and many state income tax laws. This diminishes the cost of borrowing funds.

HELOC loans are also advantageous because of the dual flexibility in terms of borrowing at will and repaying the loan according to the borrower's availabilities. This is an expert transaction for financing emergency situations, solidifying debts, property renovations, paying college tuitions, or funding a rehab or nursing home stay for an elderly parent. In other words, you borrow and pay interest exclusively on the money you need. Furthermore there are HELOCs that can be converted to a fixed-rate loan at the time of a drawing. This can be a fruitful alternative if a borrower needs to draw a sizeable sum at a given time. It's about knowing how to always have money in your hand to avoid more serious penalties that result by not having it.

C Corps Versus S Corps in the Money-Making Game

C Corporations

C corporations are standard business corporations with no liability for shareholders in which partners are taxed according to specific guidelines based on profit. They tend to conjure up large-scale images of Fortune 500 companies like Exxon Mobile and General Electric with an employee roster numbering thousands and annual revenues totaling millions if not billions of dollars. However, the truth is that C corps are advantageous even for smaller operations because doing business as a C corp allows the corporation a

100-percent employee health insurance deductible, which also covers shareholders and the cost of medical reimbursement plans. Furthermore, operating as a C corp allows fringe benefits deductions defined as tuition fees, transportation perks (i.e., company cars and passes for public transportation), and group life insurance within a $50,000 range for each employee.

Additionally, a special tax rate is applied to profits of a C corp. For example, a 15-percent rate is affixed to the first $50,000 in annual profits. In contrast, most earnings in that bracket are taxed at 28 percent. If after paying all expenses, including but not limited to employee salaries, the corporation shows a profit, then a tax payment is required, and if the profits are received as a shareholder, the dividends are taxable. This is categorized as double taxation—the grouping of a corporate income tax and a personal income tax.

In the case of a small business, often a minimum—if any—profit is shown after expenses and salaries have been deducted. This exempts the business from double taxation. In the event of a loss claim, it remains in the C corp and is not put on the shareholders' shoulders. A C corporation can carry tax losses to different years to obtain a refund.

S Corporations

On the other hand, an S corporation, which is set up for sole proprietorship or partnership and is taxed accordingly, has no Fortune 500 status because in order to conduct business as an S corp, it can not boast more than 75 shareholders. The benefit of an S corp is that there is no double taxation. The IRS grants a special tax designation for an S corporation. The election of this designation permits the corporation's profits to be the tax responsibility of the shareholder in lieu of the corporation. The benefit to operating as an S corp is that the double tax exemption would qualify as a major advantage.

Eliminating corporate net income and payment and factoring in corporate dividend income results in big tax dollar savings. Furthermore, in the event of financial loss, the responsibility is transferred to the shareholder (at least in part) offering a deduction that can lower the tax on other income.

It is not complicated to elect S-corp status for a business. The federal government provides a form 2553, which can be completed and mailed or faxed within a given time frame that does not exceed 75 days of the incorporation of the business.

Real Estate Professional Tax Deductions

Here is where your quest to become the most knowledgeable REALTOR® in the business really pays off. You have gathered all the tax data necessary to help your clients find that extra cash needed to purchase their dream home. Thanks to your dollar-saving tips, they were able to upgrade their lifestyle with a bigger and more expensive house. Consequently you are now the best agent in the world.

The client is thrilled and has taken a handful of your cards to pass along to their friends and family. Your commission check has an extra digit and your phone is ringing with referrals.

Great—but let's take it a step further and think about taxes. Larger earnings equate with higher taxes, right? You were conscientious about saving money for others, but what about for your own investment portfolio—is it growing in leaps and bounds or is it all going to Uncle Sam?

You need to be aware of the tax deductions applicable to real estate professionals. There are several categories of expenditures that qualify for tax deductions:

- **Professional Fees and Association Dues**—This includes writing off any and all costs relating to professional organizations such as the Board of REALTORS®, networking organizations like the Chamber of Commerce, as well as any fees required for obtaining or renewing a license.

- **Training Seminars and Continuing Education Courses**—If up-to-date learning is required for license renewal or to better your earning potential as an agent, the cost of getting the additional training is tax deductible. This includes all training and testing materials.

- **Business Expenses**—Besides the basic deductions of business supplies such as computer software programs, lock boxes, lawn signs, fax materials, business cards, and stationary paper, as well as film and/or digital cameras, there are advertising, appraisal, and attorney costs that can be deducted. Don't forget that there are other tax write-offs to take into consideration: computer database subscription fees, bank charges, referral fees, errors and omission and liability insurance premiums, MLS fees, legal costs, open house expenses, and gifts for clients who have closed on your listing.

- **Transportation Fees**—You should keep a log of the miles you drive during actual business, including showing property and all travel related to a transaction. This does not include commuter miles to and from your residence. For example—you can take off client, mortgage brokers, and escrow meetings as well as caravans, and travel to and from seminars, continuing education courses, and out-of-town business trips. Be conscientious about collecting and holding onto all receipts for gas, oil changes, vehicle repairs, registration, insurance, car washes, and car loan interest payments. Document all business trips according to date, destination, event, and miles traveled.

- **Out-of-Town Business Travel**—These deductions include actual air or road travel costs, meals, hotel accommodations, and reasonable expenses like car rental, public transportation, and tips to hotel employees. Keep an accurate log with receipts, and itemize carefully because some deductions—such as meals—are only 50-percent deductible.

- **Home Office Expenses**—This category covers telephone expenses—local, long distant, cellular, and credit card calls—as well as faxes, calculators, cameras, copiers, recorders, pagers, and computers. Furthermore it includes mortgage interest payments, property tax, homeowners' insurance, HOA fees (if applicable), maintenance and repairs, and utilities—electric, gas, and water.

- **Interest**—Mortgage interest on business personal and real property (with the exclusion of personal residence) and interest paid on borrowed money for the purpose of satisfying ordinary and necessary business expenses are generally tax deductible. Document all credit card finance charges used to pay for qualified business expenses, line of credit interest expenses, and any additional expense incurred as real estate professional expenses.

Although these expense categories are legitimate business expenditures, investigate them further or consult a tax professional to verify eligibility for additional deductions. Different lifestyles and business methods may provide further beneficial tax savings. This is why I say *education...education...education!* Make it a goal to both get it and give it. In return you will see your own nest egg appreciate.

9

Income Appreciation

"Every day, you'll have opportunities to take chances and to work outside your safety net. Sure, it's a lot easier to stay in your comfort zone…in my case, business suits and real estate…but sometimes you have to take risks. When the risks pay off, that's when you reap the biggest rewards."

—Donald Trump

Much to my surprise, I have discovered that most real estate agents are not property owners. It's difficult to sell something unless you are able to fully, firmly believe in the value of ownership. To know about property acquisition, you have to purchase a house.

Believing in the process and being a firsthand participant influences your sales approach. When I am looking to buy or sell my own properties, one of the first questions I ask REALTORS® is; "Do you own your home or investment property?" If the answer is no, then I find another agent because there is no way that an agent who doesn't own property can know what it takes. Moreover, if they haven't experienced it themselves, it is unlikely they will be able to satisfy my requirements and help me accomplish my purchasing objectives.

Above all, a nonowner agent is clueless about the fears and concerns of a homebuyer—especially a first-time buyer. However if the client is geared toward investing in an income-producing property, the educated agent will be able to discuss the tax benefits even if they have not personally been involved because they have investigated the allowable tax deductions. It's one thing to be able to hold on to an extra $50,000 in yearly income and another actually to have the money in your hands.

It's the same with being a landlord. Without the experience, you will be incapable of discussing tenant issues like late rental payments, property damage, and eviction notices. Would you be able to advise a client how to evict a tenant without taking the costly legal path? You would if you were a landlord who had been faced with a negligent tenant! Experience is one of the best teachers, and the more educated you become as an agent, the more trust you will build in your business. You will inspire security and clients will feel safe knowing you know more than they do.

Of course, you probably won't be excited to pay your REALTOR® a big commission if you realize that you know more and work harder on a transaction than the agent you've chosen for your investments. Nevertheless, if you can offer information and are in a position to educate a buyer *because of your experience as a buyer,* your clients will know you earned every penny of your commission.

This is why I advise all REALTORS® to get in the game and become active investors and property owners. They must be able to sniff out a great deal for themselves before they will be qualified to follow a good scent for a client. Selecting a good investment means being able to discern if it's a buyer's or seller's market because knowing how to buy wisely equates with property appreciation—and property appreciation leads to income appreciation.

Statistically speaking, property values rise over a period of time. Money is lost only when property is sold in a soft market. Yet only someone who holds a deed would be knowledgeable enough to know that investors wade through the cycles and don't sell the moment the values turn south. This same principle holds true for the stock market. A noninvestor would advise selling when the stock price begins to slip, instead of sitting out the bear moment until the bulls return.

An agent should invest in property because it is important for agents to invest their commission checks in property-acquisition money-making ventures. It is far more opportune to sell an idea or business plan you are part of and firmly believe in. If you are hesitant and afraid to use your knowledge and experience for your own financial gain this insecurity will carry over to your clients. However, if you are involved in the real estate game, you will project an empowered image of a successful investor promoting what has already been proven to be a great money-making proposition. Look at it from the client's perspective: If you're not in the game, then why should the client play?

If you attend training seminars, follow continuing education courses, and are fully equipped to assist your clients in the property investment, why not return the favor to yourself? One of the best ways to watch your income appreciate is to become an investor. The experience puts you in a great position to explore market values, comps, and the endless listings for your clients and yourself. In addition, if you want to generate a sizeable income, you must focus on clients interested in multiproperty acquisition. Learn how to do business with this type of upper-echelon investor by turning your commission checks into high-yield property investments.

Real estate is still one of the most feasible investment strategies. If investors pay attention to market trends during acquisition, investing in real estate can reap lucrative benefits. Moreover, as I've just discussed, there are many tax incentives and a rather minimum risk of loss. Most importantly, the return on the investment is potentially very high as property bought in a buyer's market rarely—if ever—does anything but appreciate in value.

Zero Dollar Investing:
The No-Down Payment Deal

Despite some sporadic fluctuations in softer markets, in a real estate market in which listing prices have appreciated, it can often be difficult if not impossible, to get your hands on the 20 percent needed to satisfy the down payment requirement. Still, though it may not have been true decades ago, in the 21st century, property can be acquired with no money down. Today, mortgage companies provide unconventional no-down payment programs and second mortgages to absorb the amount of a down payment. These programs include:

- **No-Down Payment Mortgage**—With this type of financing, 100 percent of the property purchased is financed with a single mortgage. The buyer is responsible for making a monthly mortgage payment. This is beneficial in an escalating market advantage because it permits the buyer to jump into the market without having to hold off or sacrifice beyond reason until she has the money for a down payment.

- **Second Mortgage**—This is another possibility open to investors unwilling or unable to put a down payment on a desired property. Sometimes a second mortgage is referred to as a piggyback loan. Often an 80/20-loan is applied in which 80 percent of the property cost is financed through the first mortgage and the other 20 percent via a second mortgage. This strategy is beneficial because it absolves the buyer from funding private mortgage insurance.

Prior to exercising a no-down payment loan option, it is wise to consider your actual financial situation and the status of the housing market. In a seller's market with escalating property values, it may be opportune to take advantage of a rising price trend and get in while appreciation is still occurring. However, it is prudent to evaluate and research the transaction carefully before committing. If you sign for a no-down payment mortgage and the market fluctuates toward a price decrease, you could end up owing more than the possible resale value of the house. Study the trends, meet with different lenders to ask questions, and listen to all the options available before putting your name on a contract.

Rental Property Income: Asset Appreciation

Acquiring property and leasing it to a tenant is a great way to generate income. The tenant will contribute to the mortgage payments, taxes, insurance premiums, and general maintenance fees. In order to break even, however, you must do the math before setting the rental value.

A smart property owner will calculate expenses and factor in a small profit margin. Once the mortgage is satisfied, a high percentage of the rent is turned into income. Additionally, if purchased wisely in a buyer's market, the property has appreciation potential and has probably increased in value during the mortgage payment process. Researching property values during the past few decades will give you an idea of the long-range trend of escalating home prices. Consequently the property owner ends up with an increased value asset.

In the majority of cases, those who invest in income-producing properties operate on cash flow and factor in rental income as income. They deduct expenses as they receive the rent check. Different things qualify as taxable income. Payment on a broken lease qualifies as taxable income, but a returned security deposit doesn't. If circumstances warrant keeping the security deposit due to property damage or failure to honor the conditions stipulated in the lease, this is headlined as taxable income. If the security deposit satisfies the last month's rent obligation, it is classified as income upon receipt.

Rental Income Tax Deductions

One of the positive aspects of real estate investing is the tax deductions based upon property you own. Investigate the possibilities and learn how to implement them to your own benefit.

There are numerous expenditures that are tax deductible from your rental income, including:

- **Depreciation**—Depreciation refers to the annual income-tax deduction that grants the recuperation of the cost and other basics related to tangible property (not land) for the duration of time in which you utilize the said property. In a sense it is like an expense account to compensate for natural wear and tear (appliances and furnishing) and time/climate-induced deterioration. Obsolescence is also factored in when property and conditions become outdated. The IRS has a special form 4562 to report depreciation.
- **Maintenance and Operating Fees**—Be it a single-family dwelling, a townhouse, or a network of condos, property ownership is a tax-advantage investment with different levels

of commitment to maintenance and management. Property that is purchased for rental income is considered a business. You receive revenue from the tenant's monthly rent check and you sustain expenses from the maintenance and operation of the property. Over a period of time, the revenue will probably exceed the expenses rendering cash flow to compensate for the investment in time and money. Furthermore an increase in property values is also projected over a period of time. The IRS can actually be a catalyst to income appreciation by allowing tax benefits.

- **Mortgage Points**—All of the points paid on any mortgage or loan of an income-generating property are tax deductible. Furthermore if the said property is sold, and the mortgage balance is satisfied early, the unused mortgage points for that year are tax deductible.

Other investment possibilities are:

- **Real Estate Investment Groups**—Similar to mutual funds for rental properties, with this type of investing you can purchase a rental income property without the obligation of assuming landlord responsibilities. The way this works is that a company will purchase or construct a set of apartment blocks or condominiums and then open them to investors. Investors can buy them through the company hence becoming associated with a group. Either one or multiple units can be bought and the company acting as the real estate investment group assumes operating and management responsibilities as well as maintenance. The group also takes on the marketing when leases are terminated. In recompense, the group takes a percentage of the monthly rent.

- **REITs**—Real estate investment trusts (REITs) are Wall Street's way to flip real estate into a publicly traded tool. A REIT is built on an investor's money and utilized by either a corporation or trust to buy and operate properties. They are bought and sold on the major exchanges in the same way stocks are traded. The corporation is responsible for 90 percent of the taxable profits—dividends in order to maintain the investment as a REIT. In so doing, the REIT is exonerated from corporate income taxes. Similar to most dividend-paying stocks, REITs are a solid investment and produce a dependable income.

There are many investment options open to agents. Once you are licensed and ready to prospect for clients, it is wise to practice your professional skills on yourself. Research a property, show it, make an offer, have it inspected, close your own deal, and as a property owner pay yourself a commission. Now watch it appreciate as you continue to invest in the market that allowed you to invest in the first place!

10

It Sounds Too Good to Be True—Is It Legal?

Although most agents have neither legal degrees nor membership status on the state bar, they can exercise due diligence in proving to their clients that too-good-to-be-true possibilities are perfectly legal. The most creative aspects of the real estate business are often sidestepped because REALTORS® fail to understand the value (or legality) of unconventional transactions.

I recommend getting together a team of professionals—an attorney, a CPA, and a tax specialist—with whom you can consult. Ask questions and listen to your clients. Be open to their outside-of-the box thinking venues, and be knowledgeable enough to feel comfortable and secure in opting for alternative strategies that may not be included in broker licensing courses. This will widen your field of possibilities and lead to more closings.

Client Penalty

Agents seem to think that if a resource or solution sounds too perfect, it can't be legal. The only result of this faulty thinking is what I call "client penalty." Client penalty means avoiding certain strategies that in the end prevent the client from closing the transaction. The deal was lost, a buyer came away from the negotiating table without the property, and the agent returned home without the commission check.

This is why agents need to do their homework, get the legal advice, and use it to help the client get the desired property. Turn client penalty and no commission into client satisfaction, potential referrals, and a commission check.

REALTOR® Fallacy: "It's Not Legal"

Many times agents will take it upon themselves to tell their clients "It's not legal!" However, agents are often wrong—and clients often believe them. Many opportunities are missed because clients don't ask agents for confirmation through a legal resource or reference.

- **Fallacy:** It's not legal to have the seller carry any financing whatsoever.
- **Truth:** It's perfectly legal beyond a doubt to negotiate a seller carryback because it is the lender who determines the loan conditions and exactly what a buyer is allowed to do in the

transaction. Not only is it legal to have sellers carry financing, but they can also credit money toward the closing fees, the inspection, the maintenance, and rehabbing such as painting and flooring upgrades.

Agents should pay particular attention to all offers presented. Some will be contingent upon satisfying specific financing requirements. Ask for the lender's information. This will allow you to contact the broker or lender personally to find out if the program will perform according to the buyer's claims.

Sometimes during the course of the loan process, the agent may allow something that is perhaps underwritten in a different manner. You cannot always satisfy the REALTOR'S® requests because the circumstances in the transaction are often different or have changed. Have all the facts handy.

I once negotiated a six-percent credit as the buyer. This strategy was met with insinuations from other agents that I was treading on illegal territory and would never be able to get six percent from the seller because the lenders would not permit it. I proved them wrong! Once my requests were agreed to because the legality was no longer disputed, I went ahead and signed the listing agreement, closed the deal, and deposited my commission check calculated on six percent.

The truth is that many of these individuals have not been in a situation actually to experience the process. There are numerous lenders willing to authorize a 6-percent credit. Before shouting "it's not legal," and risking forfeiture of the deal, get informed.

The Multimillion-Dollar Question: Is It Legal?

Ask the question, but don't stop there. Get the answer.

Is it legal? Is flipping property an ethical approach to income appreciation? Can a client purchase a property today, turn around, and sell it tomorrow at a higher price? Every individual attributes his own value to a property regardless of the comps. The MLS is far from the supreme authority on listing prices; and an agent's opinion does not set the house pricing market.

If a property is listed at $500,000 in the MLS and a buyer's offer of $475,000 is accepted, there is no law that states he cannot turn around and flip it for $520,000 the day after the closing.

In this scenario, the buyer behaved properly. He created an opportunity to sell the property at a higher value simply because in his mind it was worth more than the actual listing price—even if he negotiated a lesser price.

Consider that appraisers usually follow different guidelines when appraising property. This is the reason why it is important to be mindful that buyers and sellers establish market value—not the appraiser. Therefore it is not illegal to demand a higher price for an already appraised property.

Not too long ago, I listed a property for about $1 million in excess of the appraisal figure. Most of the area REALTORS® expressed their disapproval, phoning my office to remind me I was dreaming if I thought I would actually get a contract on the property. I was told financing would not be feasible at that price range. Nevertheless, I allowed myself to visualize an all cash deal.

Their reasoning was linked to the area comps theory of setting value to property. Yet my way of thinking did not factor in comps. Instead I followed my own inclination: For every property, there is a buyer. I saw value in the property far beyond what the comps determined, and if I was able to spot this value, then I was certain someone else would too.

I took the chiding and opposition in stride, and two months later had a buyer who agreed to purchase the property in an all-cash transaction. I was paid $1 million more than the MLS listed price based on area comps and an appraisal. Furthermore the buyer did a property flip and sold the house within a six-month period for $300,000 more than he paid for it!

Was it legal? You bet! Was a profit made? Absolutely! You can rightfully ask whatever you want for your property regardless of the market value, especially if the neighborhood is mixed instead of track homes. In track-home areas it is somewhat more difficult to appreciate your home's value personally.

Property acquisition is not exclusively a business investment; it is also an emotional experience for many people. Some buyers want what they want and are willing to pay a steep price to purchase their dream home. This category of buyer usually sees the same value in the property that the seller does and will not walk away from the deal if a counteroffer is rejected. Perhaps she is interested in the area schools or maybe the property is just too overwhelming to pass up. Maybe the house is adjacent to other family members, maybe it has spectacular curb appeal, or perhaps it is the best house out of 20 or 30 homes that the buyer previewed and a green light flashed when she crossed the entry threshold. Whatever the reason, the house sells above the comps, MLS, and appraiser value.

Pricing Pyramid

Many brokers depend on the pricing pyramid and believe it is a fail-proof model, so they base their appraisals on neighborhood comps. However, a savvy seller's agent is always one step ahead. Having an updated and sophisticated knowledge base is of vital importance when setting a value to a home. It is not always easy, but a faulty calculation can make the difference between a quick sale and a lingering property. Always keep in mind that the feasible dollar value of a property is the actual cash amount a buyer is wiling to pay. Everything else is secondary.

As a seller's agent, however, you have to get it right the first time or risk having a long-standing listing—or losing the listing altogether.

I recommend aiming high. Price the property at a value you feel is right, regardless of the market trends. The client should be involved and participate in the selling process. Inform the client of the area comps and market value and ask if he wants to take a stab at a higher listing price. After a specific agreed upon period of time, if there are no bites, the client should be informed that perhaps it would be more opportune to reduce the price in order to speed up the process. Once a seller decides to reduce the price, he should be advised to approach you for an expert opinion on how to price it for a profitable sale in a short period of time.

There are two ways of attacking the pricing process. You can set a property value according to the comps or lower and sell it quickly or you can hold out for a higher value and risk not selling it—or coming away with a huge profit as an award for courageous pricing.

Sometimes sellers have an inflated concept of their property's worth. Buyers might not see the same value and they'll show little interest in the property. Consequently the finger is pointed at the agent who now has to explain to the seller that the price was exaggerated for the market. This controversy leads to seller-agent loss of confidence. As a result the agent looses the listing because the seller is frustrated by the yo-yo game and seeks another REALTOR®. It could have all been avoided had the property been correctly priced for the specific market.

Soaring Above the Curve

A savvy agent will be able to get a feel for the market and understand which tactic to pursue in order to get the best deal. In today's fast-paced and high-tech real estate market, it takes a more-than-competent agent to compete and excel. Therefore, weaning yourself off the introductory "real estate for dummies" manuals is essential. Be creative. Remember that today's buyers know what they want. It's up to you to show them how they can get it.

This is why my seminars and training courses emphasize staying ahead of the game by participating in continuing-education courses that teach you how to apply *avant-garde* strategies and techniques—even those you once thought were illegal. Don't be afraid to try something different to close a deal. It's not illegal to sell a property for what you think it is worth.

Defining Legality

One way to build a reputation as an elite REALTOR® is to create solutions for clients who find themselves unable to deal with financial challenges. However, before suggesting creative approaches to financing, agents must be forthcoming and willing to learn how to leverage their business models to profit clients.

Top agents excel by introducing an innovative transaction: seller financing. Not only is this legal, it is also beneficial to both buyer and seller. Seller financing:

- Reduces the market lingering factor—the property moves quickly from listing to closing;
- Allows the property to sell for a higher value because the seller is holding a note at a lower interest rate;

- Creates lower mortgage payments for the buyer;
- Benefits the seller by offering an investment-benefit from the mortgage; and
- Permits an installment sales tax deferment in some cases.

I would define as legal anything and everything that a buyer and seller are willing to shake hands on in order to successfully close on a purchase contract. Usually the conditions established by the involved parties are technically legal as long as no federal stipulations are infringed upon regarding tax reporting and correct deed documentation and registration. In other words, it's all legal as long as the transaction is conducted above the table.

Don't judge a strategy to be illegal just because you don't understand its operating mechanism and cannot see the potential in closing the deal. Negotiation is always a powerful tool, one that can rarely be omitted from the process. Items such as furniture, appliances, and even a swimming pool are all negotiable. A buyer and seller can agree on the removal of the pool or on completing roof repairs or kitchen upgrades before closing. In addition, a certain amount of money can be deducted after the inspection report is received to allow for certain repairs. In another scenario the buyer and seller can agree to a "sold as-is" transaction. Interestingly enough, even no-money-down transactions, which most agents seem to consider shady if not downright illegal, are legal.

Whatever conditions or terms about the property and the financing program are set in writing are legally binding.

More Creative Financing Strategies

Existing Finance Transaction. An existing finance transaction removes the burden of monthly mortgage payments from a property owner who has financial restraints and could possibly risk a foreclosure. Once a title check determines that the value of the property is less than the amount owed, a buyer can take over the seller's financial responsibility. Many agents believe the "existing financing" transaction falls outside the limits of legality because of a "due-on-sale" clause. In my career as a REALTOR®, I have seen a plethora of loan documents the majority of which contain the clause "the lender may call the loan"—not *will* call the loan—if title is transferred in a transaction subject to existing financing.

In the State of California, the Association of REALTORS'® contracts include a clause that specifically states: "Are you taking this with conventional financing or subject to the existing financing?" Although California is just one state, I am certain there are many more contracts formulated with a similar clause.

If you opt to go the route of financial creativity, be conscientious about completing the appropriate documentation. Documenting "subject to existing financing" transactions requires you to understand the components of the approach. With an attorney and the correct documentation, title, loan, and all insurance can be transferred. Best of all, the client is protected—and it is all totally legal!

All-Inclusive Deed of Trust. Another transaction frequently misjudged to be illegal is the all-inclusive deed of trust, or AIDT. With an AIDT, also known as a wraparound mortgage, a loan is assumable subject to the lender's discretion. A financial program is structured to allow refinancing of an existing mortgage plus the borrowing of extra funds subject to an interest rate that fluctuates between the old loan rate and the present market rates. In this type of financing, the lender is agreeable to transferring some of the loan payments to the original mortgage lender, and wraps the remainder of the previous loan with the new loan. The borrower's obligation consists of one monthly payment.

In this transaction, the loan on an existing property is assumed and the seller creates a new loan, which wraps in her equity to the existing conventional financing.

Next a servicing agreement is drawn up with the bank that allows the buyer to pay money into a bank account. In turn, the bank, acting as the servicing company, pays the underlying mortgage and forwards the rest of it (i.e., the profit) to the seller. This method assures the buyer that her payment is tracked at the bank.

Once the purchase agreement is free of contingencies, the parties are ready to move toward closing the transaction. When all closing fees are determined, the seller can anticipate credits from the purchaser that increase the sales price of the property. The most important credit is the tax proration, which is recompense appropriated to the seller by the buyer of a percentage of the property taxes paid by the seller to cover the year preceding the sale. Credits are not limited to taxes but can be applied to homeowner and association dues, paid-in-advance service contracts, and unconsumed utilities such as heating fuel.

Seek Legal Counsel. My seminars instruct agents to advise their clients to consult and engage an attorney during the contract signing to ensure that they are putting their signature on a transaction they fully understand and are in total agreement with.

Always exercise complex transactions with the backing of legal counsel. If your company does not provide this service, it may be a wise decision to retain a qualified attorney with real estate expertise to consult for legal resources and options. He will be better-equipped to provide you with more innovative solutions for creative financing strategies.

It's All Legal. All these strategies are creative paths to the closing table. However, no matter how innovative and resourceful they may seem, they are legal. Investors are often looking for deals in which the seller is agreeable to maintaining the existing financing, and sellers often prefer to keep the financing in place to reap tax benefits.

Furthermore agents claim there is no way clients can carry paper on a property and create a second or third because in purchasing a new property they need every financial resource they have to close the deal. In addition they are completing a 1031 exchange and claim they cannot carry financing. This is erroneous thinking because in doing a 1031 exchange a client can certainly carry financing on a property as long as the money that is not applied to the exchange is subject to a different tax scale—but always legal.

The Broker Guru: Real Estate *Bravura*

I have spoken with the presidents of many REALTOR® boards and I've come away shocked to discover how many agents are unaware of what they can and cannot do. This ignorance is unfair to sellers because it prohibits many transactions from reaching closings. It also prevents buyers from purchasing their dream homes and serious investors from increasing their property holdings. Though strategies exist that sound too good to be true, we are so geared to easy living that we ironically question the validity of something that appears to be obstacle-free.

By so doing we force others and ourselves to forfeit potentially lucrative possibilities to increase our net worth because we just don't get it. This is why agents should check with an attorney specialized in real estate law *prior* to discarding a creative solution.

Of course, if an attorney red-lights your unorthodox strategy, my advice is to find one who will give the green light. Many times, a second opinion is the better opinion.

Furthermore, learning some creative strategies can benefit your personal investment projects. You could discover that you are eligible for tax benefits that you never imagined, and as an owner of an income-producing property for a lengthy period of time, when and if you opt to sell it you would be able to create a rate of return better than any financial institution would offer by carrying back the financing.

You could also decide to loan the money at a 10–15-percent interest rate and have a deferred installment sale. This enables you to defer from taxes the portion of the money you are lending. Your tax obligation covers only the money passed to you. There are formulas to assist in the calculation. This is why it is important to consult professionals—in this case, a CPA. Find out the numbers and apply them to your benefit.

Stay ahead of the game, investigate creative solutions, and learn what is legal and just how far you can stretch the limits of legality to escalate your value as a REALTOR® and appreciate your income from increased business. Present yourself with the necessary documentation to demonstrate to your clients that you are exercising your profession within full legal parameters.

Here it is wise to differentiate between *being* a REALTOR® and *succeeding* as a REALTOR®. The key is to take time to investigate resources and learn how to structure inventive—if not necessarily original—solutions not only to save the sale, but also to leave the title company with the most substantial commission check imaginable. This will not occur unless or until you feel knowledgeable and secure enough in your profession to step outside the box.

Agents should exercise due diligence when structuring transactions and be open to broad unconventional solutions. Remember the objective is to satisfy the client, build a referral base, run to the bank with a sizeable commission check, and become a profit center.

- Get moving
- Change your thinking
- Ask questions
- Attend seminars
- Consult other professionals

Gain bravura and when you step up to bat do it as a seasoned guru, not a first-day-on-the-job rookie!

11

Rehab Your Mind-set to Rehab Your Bank Account

"They can because they think they can."

—Virgil

This book has touched upon many business strategies and expounded upon some of my personal concepts with the intention of showing you how to succeed in the real estate profession, gain top-notch status as an agent, and begin to accumulate wealth. Although it is important to master business strategies, client prospecting techniques, investment options, and customer service *savoir-faire,* these factors are not sufficient to win the money-making game.

If your objective is to close more deals, collect and deposit more commission checks, invest your earned income, and watch your investments appreciate, it is necessary to rehab your mind-set by working with your intentions because intentions are the energy that empowers you. They are, in essence, the merger between wishes and resolve. Desiring something does not come with the iron-clad guarantee for attaining it unless you program your will toward moving forward to get it.

Change: The Ultimate Rehab Tool

In order to rehab an old mind-set successfully, it takes a strong will, determination, persistence, and the courage to change with a positive attitude and a firm conviction.

The majority of people I meet through my seminars and training courses respond to my suggestions of change by telling me it is difficult to put into motion and can be frightening. I reassure them by asking why they make it such a complicated task when it only takes an instant for a change to take place!

If you think about it, some individuals who have been alcoholics for decades have gone dry in the time it takes to pour and drink a glass of wine! This sends a message that if you make up your mind to break a pattern then you will set yourself in a position to make the appropriate decision and change the conditions and circumstances that prevent you from achieving your goal. You have the power to review your situation, assess the options, and decide on the choices.

How you think influences what you will accomplish. You have two possibilities: construct your own paved brick road with an easy, untroubled passage to your destination or build an obstacle course filled with detours, barriers, and dead-end streets that lead nowhere.

If your goal is to be successful doing what you love while using and developing your natural talents, then step up and choose it. Do what it takes to accomplish your goal. Seed the choice in order to reap the possibility to make that choice in your subconscious; then act on it.

Mental Makeover

Rehabbing your mind-set is about you and the power of your intentions. Teach yourself to assume productive outcomes. Positive affirmations bring optimism and constructive outcomes into your life. Restrictive beliefs do just that—they hamper and prevent you from reaching your destination. If you continue to trust that money does not sprout on trees, you will be shackled by your conviction. This type of silent brainwashing that remains trapped in the subconscious expands and manifests itself in a deficient and restricted lifestyle.

You can reverse the course of your life by getting a complete mental makeover. Learn how to take inventory of your success-restraining thoughts. Reevaluate and rehab your conscious mind to get what you truly desire instead of concentrating on what you have or don't have. Eliminate the toxic words. Edit your mind's vocabulary to replace "I can't" with "I can" and "I will." Always be in full control of your thoughts and attentive to what will prevent you from achieving an objective. Remake your thoughts one by one until they have the power to give you what you want. Above all *never expect or accept a refusal, denial, or no.*

Learn self-motivation and gain the knowledge to expand your vision. Minds are like computers; although they have been programmed, they can be reformatted and reprogrammed. Best of all, you can reprogram your mind with any data you wish, as long as you truly desire it. It is not an easy process because it takes energy and commitment. Not everyone is a multimillionaire; it takes incredible effort to succeed. Of course, this doesn't mean that you can't join the list if you commit to changing your way of thinking!

Believe It—Achieve It

You might be tempted to think that mind-set doesn't matter—it's all just pretence—but instead consider it a reality. In so doing, you will eventually come to the realization that what you think about is what you bring about. The is a potent vehicle for progress. If a substantial bank account and professional clout are your objectives, you need to rev-up your energy with positive thoughts.

In essence, you already have the resources to be in command and surpass obsolete and dysfunctional concepts that get in the way of your success. Assume control of your life by accepting that what you think about is what you bring about and what you focus on will expand.

Visualize It—Realize It

It is essential to understand that you create and become what you are able to perceive. Likewise, what you cannot visualize, you will neither become nor accomplish. Projection is the secret to achievement. Rehab your mind, reprogram it to visualize how successful you want to be, and how much money you want to earn. Then see yourself as a participant in the scenario you created in your mind. Read the script and play the part. Be the protagonist in your own dream. Don't just sit in the audience as a spectator observing others win the prizes.

Involve yourself in your vision. Watch as you shake hands with a client who just closed on your multimillion-dollar property listing. Notice the business card in her hand—hear her excited words as she tells you that a friend of hers is interested in listing an apartment complex with you. Step into the scene—feel the rush of adrenaline as you imagine your potential earning. How does walking in the shoes of a top-notch REALTOR® resonate with you?

Projection is like a trial run, a kind of tryout that allows you to visualize what it feels like to star in your ideal role. Running through the scenario in your mind will give you the opportunity to inquire if you feel at ease with the responsibility your role presents. It will get you to question if you can handle the increased wealth and accept account-ability for your new status.

Challenge yourself to move ahead. Visualize yourself climbing up a ladder without an end to reach as far as the stars. In my lectures, I often refer to my "step up" motto—decide where your next level will be, then step up to it, step into it, and show up to step up!

Switch into fast-forward and daringly envision yourself stepping onto higher ground and abandoning the mediocre patchiness you may have accepted from yourself. It's over—you have rehabbed your mind-set.

Everyone knows when they are reluctantly settling for something, accepting a given situation or set of conditions, fully cognizant that they are capable of producing a more profitable outcome. When you are certain you can achieve more, but choose not to, you are not the author of your own choices. Instead, you are deleting your intention, reversing your course, and setting yourself in a position to be governed by extraneous forces.

Take responsibility; be conscious of the fact that this is your choice exclusively. You will fall into it neither blindly nor compromisingly, and as a result of your decision, you will create the life you visualize in your dreams.

Empowering Intentions

Intention is your most empowering tool. When appropriately used it has the power to infuse the mind with priceless ideas and thoughts. Intention is the pulse of your mind, the life force, the driving factor that steers it from a clear slate to a prosperous font of resources. Without intention, your mind would be an empty space: inadequate and worthless.

The power of intention is the energy that actually empowers you. It is in essence the fusion of want and resolution. Desiring something doesn't come with a guarantee of attaining it unless you program your will to get it. I like to think of intention as the gray eminence, the power behind the throne, the dynamic energy that determines if your choice will be successful or not.

I remember setting my intentions before I acquired a clear definition of what I was doing. Looking back I realize it was something I did automatically. I focused on accruing wealth through real estate and set my intention on succeeding. Now years later I can see the universal scheme of things, a plan that inspires me to recognize just how natural the laws of the universe are. Whether conscious or unconscious, the setting of an intention will result in an exhibition of that intention. That is why it is important to prioritize your wants and needs when setting intentions. Thoughts that furnish the consciousness have more startling effects on the nature of outcomes than most people realize.

When you begin to comprehend fully the power of intention, you will feel comfortable embracing the truth that you are the cause of every effect in you life. Once you've gained this insight, you will take responsibility for your actions and be accountable to yourself before completing an action. Envision living with the assurance that you can have whatever you want—all you have to do is set your intention on achieving it, and it's yours! Imagine the reality of this fantastic truth! If you want to make your wants your accomplishments, visualize embracing them.

People have the power to manifest their deepest intentions outwardly. Therefore, if you continue to envision yourself as a mediocre REALTOR® with a net earning in the five figures, chances are you will manifest that reality in your professional life and not move ahead into prospecting for more business. Eventually you'll blame a soft market for your failure to close deals and deposit commission checks.

Maybe it's time to rethink the way you approach your business and yourself. Perhaps it's unfair to find excuses for your failure to earn more money. Face it—the blame for your rookie paycheck lies in your mind. You visualize a soft market and in your subconscious, you create a reason not to do what it takes to bring in the commission checks.

Keep your mind open to the flow of positive energy. Engage yourself in a positive dialogue to reinforce your wishes and reflect your intention in the content of your words. Consequently, you will have a chance to create that all-determining "intentional power" responsible for a successful outcome.

Often fear of the new or unfamiliar intimidates, and change represents the unknown—the big question mark. It is true that change often brings discomfort, but what we sometimes fail to recognize is that the jittery nerve-wracking feeling is actually the *right way to go.* Frequently when we feel hesitant or uneasy about a new situation, deal, or client, it's probably the path we should follow.

If you always walk along the same path, you'll eventually become dissatisfied and look for another route. In order to change course you must change your intention. Don't continue to walk in your same footprints; head in another direction. Be honest with yourself and realistic about your changes.

Focus your mind-set on the intention of doing what you love to do and making what you do something you love. This will enable you to rechannel your energy to attract a different set of circumstance and scenarios. New opportunities will sprout that will grow into bigger business opportunities.

From Rookie Agent to REALTOR® Guru

Many agents operate out of fear. They shut themselves off in an earning-limited world and never try to increase the volume of their business. They are afraid of relinquishing the security blanket woven from knowing their bills will get paid. Fear of the unknown is a powerful motivator, albeit a negative one. Sometimes agents will stick to their business model because at least it guarantees them a functional income. However, is this what you really want? Are you satisfied with a rookie commission check?

Believe in yourself and face each day with the self-confidence to accept and feel comfortable with what you deserve—an abundance of wealth. Understand your passion, know what you love to do, and be reassured by the knowledge that the income you derive from doing what you're good at and like doing is well-merited. Living your life with passion and the conviction that you deserve top-notch status as a REALTOR®, makes you eligible to receive the wealth you earn.

Take inventory of your current mind-set; is it programmed for success or is it still in mediocrity mode? The wealthy mind-set converts circumstances into opportunities, whereas mediocre thinking defines everything as something that has to be done.

The big-buck thinkers have a panoramic vision. They see it; they feel it; they fully participate in it. If you ask a successful person, "How do you see the next year of your life," you will receive a vivid account with every aspect precisely detailed, down to the utmost degree because they know what they want and how to get it. Furthermore, they have set their intention on getting it. There is no rookie-agent thinking here—this is the mind-set of the REALTOR® guru—the big-commission broker who has programmed himself not only to amass commission checks but also to invest wisely and flip the dollars into a fortune.

We all have choices in life. Some people believe in accepting whatever fate deals out. Others prefer to take an active role in the design of their lives believing they know best what will make them happy. Regardless of the path you choose, you must make a decision: Will you be satisfied with what you have or would you prefer to achieve even greater success?

Make the decision, set the intention, and go for your prize!

Acknowledgements

Thank you to my wonderful agent John Willig at Literary Services Inc. for believing in this project and helping me share it with Realtors and agents worldwide.

Thanks also to the wonderful staff at Kaplan Publishing.

And special thanks to Nancy for all the hours spent in creative conversations that made this book possible.

About the Author

Tonja Demoff is a former U.S. Air Force recruiter who became a sought-after lecturer and consultant, and one of the highest-producing REALTORS® in the United States. She has founded more than 10 companies, as well as her own charitable foundation, The Tonja Demoff Foundation, which funds programs for low-income homebuyers as well as supporting community projects. A frequent radio and television guest speaker, she is a RE/MAX Hall of Fame Award winner. In 2006, Tonja was named the Top RE/MAX agent in the United States.

How to Gain Financial Freedom

One of the best ways to ensure a pipeline of valuable clients is to create a lead-generating system. Tonja Demoff's *Financial Freedom Seminars* franchise is a broad customer database and a valuable educational tool for all REALTORS® who want to cash millions of dollars in commission checks. For more information, visit her website at *www.tonjademoffcompanies.com*.

Index